Harlem Moon

Broadway Books

New York

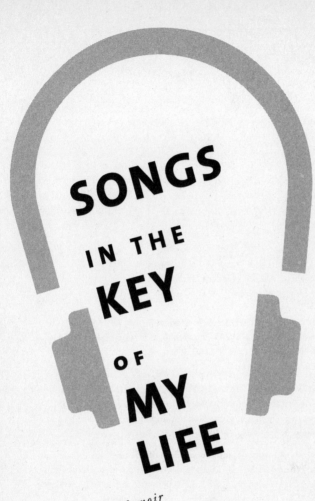

SONGS
IN THE
KEY
OF
MY
LIFE

A Memoir

FERENTZ LAFARGUE

PUBLISHED BY HARLEM MOON

Copyright © 2007 by Ferentz Lafargue

All Rights Reserved

Published in the United States by Harlem Moon, an imprint of The
Doubleday Broadway Publishing Group, a division of Random House,
Inc., New York.
www.harlemmoon.com

HARLEM MOON, BROADWAY BOOKS, and the HARLEM MOON
logo, depicting a moon and a woman, are trademarks of Random
House, Inc. The figure in the Harlem Moon logo is inspired by a graphic
design by Aaron Douglas (1899-1979).

Cataloging-in-Publication data is on file with the Library of Congress.

ISBN 978-0-7679-2406-1

PRINTED IN THE UNITED STATES OF AMERICA

10 9 8 7 6 5 4 3 2 1

First Edition

This book is dedicated to

Randy Lafargue

Georges Labossiere

Clarence A. Haynes

and

Stevie Wonder

acknowledgments

First and foremost, I want to thank my parents, Claudette and Francy Lafargue, who have been models for discipline, ingenuity, and perseverance. Without their support I would never have gotten to where I am now or where I am about to go. Aunt Bertolette, Aunt Irma, Edner, Alexande, Evens, Hardy, Jenny, and my godson Jude, my academic godparents June and Robert Bobb—thank you all for the love, laughter, and faith. *Merci bien pour toute ma famille en Haïti.*

Thank you, my lord and savior, Jesus Christ.

Special thanks to those who read drafts of chapters: Alyssa Alston, Kevin Anderson, Bernadette Atuahene, Ruth Nicole Brown, Laurel Brown, Shanique Davis, Erica R. Edwards, Javon A. Frazier, Rachel K. Ghansah, Joshua Guild, Joshua Hill Jr., Angela Hurdle, Nyasha Laing, Brian G. Lewis, Sheika Luc, Vivek Maru, Sara-Jane Mathieu, Emmanuel Raymundo, Neil Roberts, Jamila Thompson, Dorian Warren, Leslie Wingard, and The Aristocrats (Tavia N'Yongo Turkish, Robin Mookerjee, Deborah Levitt, Anne Murphy). Please keep an eye out for the work of Richard Louissaint, who took some of my author photos and who has been a unique friend for over a decade. I owe a particular debt of gratitude to Sean P. Chambers, Melanca Clark, and Lorelei Williams for taking the time to read the manuscript and their encouraging words during one marathon period of writing and worrying. All my love goes to my friends from Jamaica, Queens: Calvin Chen, Olive Chen, Miguel Correa, Blayne Erskine, Kwame Flaherty, and Cynthia Rosales.

Thank you to: *New Youth Connections*, particularly my first editor Phil Kay, for giving me an opportunity to exercise my skills as a writer and explore some of these issues as a teenager. My friends and mentors at Yale. My students and colleagues at Eugene Lang College, the New School for Liberal Arts. The BBV. My friends at Cadman Memorial Congregational Church. The Frontliners and 20/30s ministries at Emmanuel Baptist Church in Brooklyn. Thank you to the students at Dartmouth College's Cutter-Shabazz House for their hospitality and feedback during my February 2006 visit.

Thank you to Janet Hill and the staff at Harlem Moon/Random House. I look forward to future collaborations.

Thank you to all the musicians whose work appears in this project; without you none of this would be possible. Thank you for sharing your gifts with me so that I may share my story. Thank you to the editors and writers at allmusic.com, whose efforts were invaluable for securing dates for many of these memories. A special nod is extended to

Craig Werner, whose *Higher Ground* helped put Stevie Wonder's work in context, and to Nick Hornby, D. V. DeVincentis, and Stephen Frears for bringing *High Fidelity* to the screen.

I want to offer my sincerest thanks and love to Melody F. Baker. This book would not have been possible without your companionship, laughter, and vegetable curry.

There are also four people to whom this book is dedicated. First is my brother, Randy. Randy, being your brother is the greatest honor I have ever received. It has been a pleasure watching you grow and a blessing to have a brother as giving and supportive as you. I cannot say it enough: I love you.

I also dedicate this book to Georges Labossiere. Thank you for three decades of friendship. It's been a whirlwind experience watching you go from boy to man and eventually to husband and father. May God continue to bless you, Natalie, Zion, Ava, and everyone else in your family.

Third is Clarence A. Haynes. Who ever thought that "let's have lunch" could mean so much? Throughout the writings of *Songs in the Key of My Life* you have been an editor and a friend. You have been sensitive, warm, open, and—most important—honest. Thank you for challenging me to become more focused with and dedicated to my writing. I look forward to building on the lessons learned during our collaborations. You also made sharing these stories easier because of the generosity with which you shared yourself, and for that I will be eternally grateful.

And of course, this book is also dedicated to Stevie Wonder.

contents

1. INTRODUCTION: "JOY INSIDE MY TEARS" / *Stevie Wonder*

"I'm not happy."

"What do you mean?" I asked. I was sure that I'd misheard her, or that by "not happy" she meant "not happy" with the fries or "not happy" with the cold spell that we thought was uncharacteristic of southern France. Clearly she wasn't suggesting that she was "not happy" in our relationship. She was.

A little less than a year after I'd proposed to her, my fiancée, Tricia, announced she wanted to terminate our engagement. She made her declaration over lunch in the plaza in Montpellier, France, in April 2003.

I had been looking forward to traveling to France with Tricia ever since she blissfully told me about her previous time there. I thought that by experiencing Paris together, I'd experience a similar euphoria. Instead, I spent two weeks fearing my parents' and friends' reactions once I told them that Tricia and I were no longer engaged, and bracing myself for life without Tricia for the first time in five years.

Six months later in October 2003 those three words—"I'm not happy"—were still ringing in my head as I took in my new apartment. I'd lived with Tricia for one year, and now everything in the apartment was my own: the bed, the desk, the portrait on the wall—and the bills. I had discarded all the pictures of us together, the love letters written, and everything that we had bought together for our previous apartment. While I was proud that I had erased virtually all signs of her from my apartment, her presence still weighed heavily on my heart.

I was alone. When there was no more dissertation writing to be done, when I couldn't read any further and there weren't any more friends awake to talk with, I found myself in the bed alone, wondering how all this came to be.

Was my father right? Should I be ashamed that things didn't work with Tricia?

I thought about what else I could have done to make it work, or why I didn't take any number of opportunities to end the relationship for good. The deeper that I let myself fall into thought, the more I ended up crying, or rather craying, that sorrow-laden blend of crying and praying delivered in perfect pitch by those in mourning.

I crayed because I was confused, and wondered if Tricia knew that her need to find her happiness would bring about so much pain for me, and if she did know, whether she cared. This was the point where I usually broke down and my craying intensified. Regardless of whether she cared,

Tricia had the right to find her own happiness, even if that happiness didn't include me.

So I tried to muster the courage and energy to discover my own joy. One Saturday morning, I got out of bed and started ruffling through the unopened boxes piled in my living room in search of my CDs. After a few minutes of searching, I was able to cull a stack of albums by artists whose harmonies the heartbroken have been relying upon for ages: Billie Holiday, Etta James, and Nina Simone. From that point on, every Saturday morning I pulled out another batch of CDs to listen to as I went about researching and writing my dissertation.

As this ritual took form, I took to calling it church, the only word I knew which captured the sense of cleansing, praise, and rehabilitation that I was undergoing as the sounds of these artists filtered throughout my apartment. I gave some of these Saturdays special names, as is done in many Protestant congregations. On African Appreciation Day, I invited a Nigerian brother by the name of Fela Kuti to address my one-man congregation. I extended a similar invitation for Deacon Robert Nester Marley to sing a few homilies on Caribbean Appreciation Day. After these deacons and deaconesses were through leading the praise-and-worship portion of the service, that Holy Roller from Saginaw, Michigan, Reverend Steveland Hardaway Judkins would step to the podium and offer the same invocation that he offered week after week:

> *Good morn or evening friends.*
> *Here's your friendly announcer . . .*

Reverend Steveland, or Reverend Stevie as I called him back then, was installed as my pastor during my third Saturday of worship. Having been deeply moved by his sermon from the week before, I knew that his musical doxologies were exactly what I needed to hear. Once Reverend Stevie uttered the opening lines from his oration, "Love's in Need of Love Today," I settled in to hear him recite the other twenty-one sermons off his masterful 1976 double album, *Songs in the Key of Life*.

Songs in the Key of Life marked the culmination of one of the most dynamic four years of production by any musician in the twentieth century. This string began in 1972 with the arrival of both *Music of My Mind* and *Talking Book,* the second and third albums that Stevie Wonder had complete control over after renewing his Motown contract. They inaugurated the funkier blues-laden sound that Wonder became known for once he was freed from the reins of Motown's singles-driven balladeer style. The following year he unleashed *Innervisions*, and in 1974 he completed this quartet with *Fulfillingness' First Finale.*

Within four years Wonder premiered five albums, two of which—*Talking Book* and *Innervisions*—are often referred to as classics. Many consider a third, *Songs in the Key of Life*, a masterpiece, his magnum opus. The fact that a twenty-six-year-old man who had been blind since birth created such a prolific period not only reaffirmed Wonder's credentials as a prodigy but also elevated him to the level of genius.

It wasn't until Tricia and I started dating in 1998 that I really became acquainted with *Songs in the Key of Life*. It all began on a Sunday, the eve of our first day of classes at Yale, when I invited her and her roommate over for dinner.

As we ate, Tricia and her roommate got into a conversation about sampling. Tricia was critiquing Coolio's use of "Pastime Paradise," one of the tracks off of *Songs*, but she couldn't remember its name and began wading through my CD collection in search of *Songs in the Key of Life*, only to discover that it wasn't there. She thought it was a glaring omission on my part. Similarly when tracks from the album like "Ngiculela—Es Una Historia I Am Singing," "Isn't She Lovely," and "As" came on over the radio during one of our dates or manic study sessions, we'd swap memories about our earliest recollections of these songs, only to have the conversation arrested by the fact that the album wasn't there for us to listen to.

Yet the most vivid image I have about the album during the early stages of our relationship is from the first time that I went to her parents' house and saw the record's cover atop their stereo. Having never seen the cover before, I thought it was a piece of art that her parents had hung over the stereo. I was struck by the lush shades of brown and orange filling the canvas. From far away I wasn't able to tell whether the image was the center of a flower or the sun. Drawing closer I realized that it was also possible that the image was of the skyline at dusk, the sun slowly setting over the mountains in the foreground with the red sea lying slightly beyond the horizon.

This last interpretation was in line with a painting by an Eritrean artist that her parents had on the wall nearby, and since her dad was from Eritrea, I thought this was another reminder of his homeland. When I finally got close enough to read the lines in the center of the image and saw that it read, "Songs in the Key of Life. Stevie Wonder," I knew that just for the cover alone, I needed to have a copy of this record.

Noticing my fascination with the album, Tricia's mom told me that I could put it on, but I'd have to find the CD because their record player was broken. As I searched for the CD among the pile next to the stereo, she continued talking about growing up in Detroit when *Songs in the Key of Life* was first released. To my surprise, I learned that "Sir Duke" was the big hit off that album, and not "Isn't She Lovely," the infectious aria dedicated to his daughter, Aisha. Listening to her talk about "Sir Duke" and Detroit in 1976 reminded me of my own mother, who liked regaling me with stories about being in Haiti in 1976. Just like my mom, Tricia's mother spoke of being young and the thrills induced by her favorite musicians—except in conversations with my mom, these artists had names like Orchestra Tropicana, Skah Shah, and Nemours Jean-Baptiste, the Haitian equivalents to the Motown and soul legends of the '60s and '70s.

I felt at home in Tricia's parents' living room as her mom framed this album for me. Once "Sir Duke" came on, I heard in the trumpet intro sounds eerily reminiscent of the horn sections in the konpa bands whose records my parents played when I was growing up. And then Wonder sang:

> *Music is a world within itself*
> *With a language we all understand . . .*

These lyrics deftly captured my feelings while listening to *Songs in the Key of Life* in the company of Tricia and her family that evening. I was enchanted by the semblances of her father's native Eritrea in the album's artwork and how Wonder's music brought together Africa and the Americas in one glorious cavalcade of emotions, rhythms, and aspirations.

This heartening introduction to *Songs in the Key of Life* was a stark contrast to the reintroduction occurring in my own living room on Saturday mornings in the fall of 2003. My previous listens to the album had their own theme. When hanging with Tricia's family, we focused on the upbeat or sentimental selections: "Sir Duke," "Isn't She Lovely," "As," "Another Star," "If It's Magic," or "Knocks Me Off My Feet." If our conversations were more pensive, we gravitated toward "Pastime Paradise," "Village Ghetto Land," "Saturn," or "Black Man," the songs that reflected Wonder's concerns as a human rights activist.

Now that I was alone, a new set of songs with which I had never really concerned myself were taking priority. "Love's in Need of Love Today," "Ordinary Pain," "Summer Soft," and "Have a Talk with God" bewitched my imagination. "Love's in Need of Love Today," an appeal for more love in the world, directly captured my personal longing for more love, and for being in love. "Have a Talk with God" reflected the conversations with God I revived during many of my craying moments, and "Summer Soft" was particularly painful because it reminded me of and all the activities associated with our planned June 2004 wedding—sending out save-the-date cards and invitations, selecting caterers—that weren't going to happen.

Yet "Joy Inside My Tears" had the most to say. It's one of the album's slower-paced songs. It wasn't a breakout hit in the mold of "I Wish" and "Sir Duke," nor did it develop an infectious cult following like "Isn't She Lovely." Ushered in by a slow bass line that cradles the listener as the snare taps gently rock us back and forth, "Joy Inside My Tears" is one of the more subtle reflections of Wonder's musicianship. Lyrically poetic, it resonates just as clearly on the page as it does in stereo:

> You you you made life's his • to • ry
> You brought some joy inside my tears . . .

Wonder cries out his lyrics over a score that could easily have been used for a lament instead of a celebration. "Joy" touched my own sadness, helping me embrace the idea of having someone be the center of my joy while inspiring me to look beyond my romantic loss and see what parts of life I could celebrate.

As "Joy" filled my living room I realized that through music Wonder had captured my feelings about Tricia and where I was now. I began to think about what other parts of my life might've also had musical accompaniments.

There was a song coursing through every experience I'd had, from my first crush to my most significant adult relationship. It was surreal that Bone Thugs-N-Harmony's "Crossroad" was there while I consoled my brother after members of his girlfriend's family were murdered. I took glee in remembering my hot and heavy sessions with Teena Marie's "Portuguese Love." These reflections inspired me to come up with a playlist for the page, to share a batch of songs that have been there for me in all of life's permutations, which will hopefully help others reflect on their own relationships to music, and life.

In the midst of heartbreak, I found the spirit of the

writer in me that I had suppressed during my six years of graduate school. During that time, I put off exploring my interests in creative writing "until I finished my dissertation," which soon became "until I got tenure," then "until Tricia and I got settled and had kids," and more outrageously, right before we broke up, "until we could afford a summer home so that I can escape and write." For six years I put off a passion that was stirring inside of me, and were it not for that breakup, I was on the verge of putting it off for six more years and then some.

As my words filled up the page, I found myself crying again. For the first time in years I turned to poetry, adapting one of Wonder's songs, "Ngiculela—Es Una Historia I Am Singing," with the same fertile energy that I once put into remixing pop tunes for my first crush, Adriana Hernandez. I wrote in order to exercise both my talent as a writer and the spirit that I brought along with me as a child from Haiti to the United States. I wrote to explore my connection with the musical and political pulse of Africa and its diaspora. The more I wrote the more it became apparent that as the soul child of ancestors who have been making and remaking the manna of sound for ages, I am trying to do through writing what my forebears have done through music:

> *I am writing from my heart to you and yours:*
> *I am writing of love.*
> *I am writing of joy.*
> *I am writing of pain.*
> *I am writing from my heart.*
> *I am writing to my ancestors.*
> *I am writing my past so that I can right my future.*

I am writing because ma-Cine, ma-Tine, and père-Cazeau couldn't.

I am writing because boss-Justin is still around to tell me stories.

I am writing for all the elders teaching us to listen.

I am writing because sometimes I do not have the words to speak.

I am writing to my friends and family.

I am writing to those who have yet to grace this earth.

I am writing to say thank you, Stevie Wonder.

I am writing to thank him for composing Songs in the Key of Life.

I am writing him a thank-you note for helping so many of us feel right.

2. "CARIBBEAN QUEEN" / *Billy Ocean* AND "MICKEY" / *Toni Basil*

Like countless other women in the 1980s, my mother was in love with Billy Ocean. Their love affair started when *Suddenly*, the 1984 album featuring his breakout single "Caribbean Queen," was released. Whenever Ocean was on TV, Mom turned into a sixteen-year-old girl; she'd scamper into the living room with her arms flailing in the air and plop down on the couch as she bellowed out in excitement, "IS THAT HIM?" As Ocean conducted an interview or as one of his music videos played, Mom bounced up and down on the couch, pumping her fist "yes," and clapping gleefully as her "husband" spoke to her through our TV set. If it was in fact a music video, it was only a matter of seconds before she shot up off the couch to dance and sing along to her husband's video. I can still hear her singing "Caribbean Queen"

with a thick Haitian accent: "Caribbean Queen . . . boom a boom, boom. Boom a boom boom, boom . . . Caribbean Queen." The only intelligible words in Mom's rendition were the two that seemed to matter most to this woman from the islands: "Caribbean" and "Queen."

As a third grader who, believe it or not, was a budding metalhead, the last thing I wanted to do was listen to Billy Ocean, much less hear my mom butchering one of his songs. Mom may have been my only test case, but I was positive that beneath Ocean's gruff voice and the random computer-generated sounds of "Caribbean Queen" were subliminal messages instructing thirty-seven-year-old Haitian mothers on how to embarrass their young sons.

Trinidadian-born Ocean's homage to his "Caribbean Queen" oddly enough doesn't sound very Caribbean. In spite of the fact that "Caribbean Queen" was produced by another Trinidadian, Keith Diamond, the steel drum sound associated with the island's calypso music, and which permeates the recordings of balladeer and Ocean contemporary David Rudder, for example, is absent. Instead we get computer-generated sound effects that run the gamut from lasers to what sounds like a horror-movie villain's snicker. But like Ocean's other hits, "Caribbean Queen" does have a wispy bass line and jazz overtures: in this case, a saxophone solo that became the trademark of the programming lists at the adult-contemporary stations that began popping up around the country in the mid-'80s.

American audiences might not place Ocean in the same category as '80s R&B crooners Jeffrey Osborne and James Ingram, but Ocean's place alongside his American peers is well deserved. Not only was he one of the few Caribbean or black British artists to achieve success in America in the early '80s, but he was one of the most successful black artists of that era—period. "Caribbean Queen" vaulted him from competing with other black British acts for pole position at the bottom of the international charts to battling it out with established American artists.

Ocean scored many hits, including "Suddenly" in 1984, which appeared on the same album as "Caribbean Queen," "There'll Be Sad Songs (To Make You Cry)" in 1986, and "Get Outta My Dreams, Get into My Car" in 1988. Ocean's success in the '80s put him only slightly behind Mom's other husband, Lionel Richie, with whom he fought as earnestly for supremacy over the pop and R&B charts as he did for her affection—or so she alleges.

Still, even though the song initially got on my nerves, I did take serious notice of its impact on Mom, and thought that maybe another member of the opposite sex might have a similar reaction—namely, my third-grade crush Adriana Hernandez, a tall Puerto Rican princess with auburn locks and a sheepish smile. Mom's intense adoration of Billy Ocean and her connection to his song piqued my curiosity about what would happen to a girl who could understand all the lyrics and had the opportunity to sit next to a "Caribbean King" every day in class. The same spirits that previously worked Mom over finally took hold of me one day when, while listening to her singing "Caribbean Queen" for about the millionth time, I rolled off my bed, skipped my usual exasperated groan, picked up my composition notebook, and penned a ballad for my beloved Adriana:

Puerto Rican Queen,
If we're sharing the same dream
We can go and have some fun.

Puerto Rican Queen,
If we've been sharing the same dream
You'll say I'm the one.

This was a fairly easy trick for a third grader to pull off because, well, because the original song itself sounds as if it is written by a fifth grader. Days passed, and once again "Caribbean Queen" was playing in the house. As Ocean belted out the song's refrain, my mind wandered toward the way that Adriana blushed, turning her head to her left, raising her right shoulder to cover her smile. Lying there daydreaming with "Caribbean Queen" playing in the next room and Mom singing backup in the kitchen, I realized that it was about time that I presented my remix to Adriana. So after school the following day in front of Adriana's building, I presented her with a piece of paper with the ballad that I had dug deep into my heart to pen for her and proceeded to sing it for her as passionately as I imagined Ocean singing it to one of his admirers.

Adriana became almost completely overcome by laughter. The more she laughed the more effort I put into the song, belting out my lyrics for "Puerto Rican Queen" as if they were the last words I'd ever utter. When I finished she kept on laughing and was now bracing herself by holding on to my arm. Once she composed herself, she smiled and said, "You're so silly."

I thought I'd die.

None of her other "You're so sillys" ever stirred my senses like this one. I felt my stomach tingling with glee. Her wide smile was all the evidence I needed to issue Ocean a pardon for unleashing "Caribbean Queen" into the stratosphere. My heart softened and I conceded that while he may be my mother's husband, he's my main man. Staring into Adriana's brown eyes, I lost sight of the fact that my fingers no longer felt as if they were part of my hands as they flickered back and forth against my leg. Adriana and I just stood there.

Our silence was broken by the sound of her sisters, who were peeking out the window, giggling at us as they relayed a message from her mother asking Adriana to come inside. She turned around and ran into her building. When she reached the top step, she clutched the doorknob and took another look back at me. Then I began walking home.

I was so hungry to re-create this experience that as soon as I got home I scoured the record charts for another song to adapt for my muse. This time around none of my mom's other husbands helped any. Lionel, Smokey, and Marvin had nothing that I could run with. Fortunately one day while my pal Alex and I were watching my upstairs neighbor's car for him, Toni Basil's "Mickey" came on. Alex and I had tucked ourselves into the car and were taking turns sitting at the wheel, and pretending it was our ride. As we bopped along to the infectious "Mickey," some of the girls in the neighborhood strolled up to the car to check out who was inside. While Alex talked to the girls, I ran the song over and over in my mind, thinking of how to remake it for Adriana.

I shortened her name, calling her Adi like we usually did at school, and then proceeded from there:

Oh Adi, you're so fine
You send chills down my spine
Oh Adi.
Oh Adi.

For those of you who were trapped underneath a rock or living in the depths of the Amazon during the early '80s, "Mickey" was one of the catchiest songs of the decade. It was the '80s equivalent to Right Said Fred's "I'm Too Sexy" or, even better yet, Los del Rio's "Macarena." Appearing on Basil's 1981 album *Word of Mouth*, "Mickey" has a cheerleader-esque chant and pep-squad drum line reminiscent of a number that might be found in the musical *Grease*.

The syrupy high-school cheerleader chant is rather misleading. Listen to the lyrics carefully and you'll hear that the song is actually about a sexually frustrated woman abandoned yet again by her lover. As a nine-year-old, I was enthralled by the infectious chorus and unaware of the underlying meaning of lines like:

Anyway you want to do it
I'll treat you like a man . . .

Nope. I, probably like most people, simply walked around singing the chorus without giving a second thought to what the rest of the song was about. By the time that "Mickey" came out, Basil was already in her late thirties and was going into her third decade in the entertainment business. Without a catalog of hits or a breakout movie role to balance her newfound popularity, like pop peer Olivia Newton-John had, it makes sense that Basil's "Mickey," which became her only major U.S. hit, didn't lead to more success. And since she wasn't a teenybopper in real life, it would've been impossible for her to keep up this guise in the age of the music video youth movement soon to be ushered in by the likes of Cyndi Lauper, Pat Benatar, and Madonna.

Basil capitalizes on her experience as a cheerleader, dancer, and choreographer to home in on the more youthful qualities of the song.

I imagined the look that was going to overtake Adriana's face when she heard my Basil-inspired ditty. I looked forward to the thrill of her holding my arm again to brace herself.

The following Friday I presented "Adi," my cover of "Mickey," to Adriana while we were in class. After reading it she just looked up at me and again said that I was "silly." This time she said it rather matter-of-factly and with barely a hint of the glee she possessed after I sang "Puerto Rican Queen" for her.

At first I thought it was because I hadn't sung it for her. So that afternoon when we got to lunch, I sang it to her in front of her friends. As soon as I started singing, the other girls began laughing, and I kept on in anticipation that Adriana would join in. But she never laughed and instead of proclaiming me silly, she told me to quit acting silly. She grew more frustrated as the other girls, led by Adriana's best friend and my nemesis Sammi, started teasing her. "Adi's got a boyfriend," they chanted. Adriana tried telling them that I wasn't her boyfriend, which only further fueled their kidding.

Not having my wits about me, I somehow thought this was a good response and left school that day thinking I was

Adriana's boyfriend even though she hadn't spoken to me for the rest of the afternoon. Imagine my surprise when I walked into school on Monday and found out that my beloved Adriana was now the "girlfriend" of one of my friends, Eric, and they were "going out." When we settled into class that morning, I pretended to be naïve and asked Adriana about her romance with Eric:

FERENTZ: What does "going out" mean?

ADRIANA: It means he's my boyfriend.

FERENTZ: Oh, did you kiss him?

ADRIANA: Ew! hell no!

FERENTZ: Well, if he's your boyfriend, doesn't that mean you two will kiss?

ADRIANA: Uh-uh! Nope, because you can get pregnant by kissing and I don't want to get pregnant. Hey, what are you laughing at?

She punctuated her question with a punch to my left side that startled me, making me lose my breath. I composed myself and told her what my dad had told me—that you'd have to do more than kiss to get a girl pregnant. Then she stared at me. I didn't know whether she was going to commend me for sharing this information with her or punch me again, but I know that I did enjoy having her brown eyes fixed on me.

Her stare must've tickled me this time because I started giggling, slightly hiccuping through grins and clearing the way for Adriana to start talking: "If you think kissing is so fine, why don't you go and kiss him?"

"Because I want to kiss you."

I had no idea where the words came from and immediately dropped my arm to shield my left side in anticipation of the punch that was sure to follow. The punch never arrived. Suddenly I felt the butterflies in my stomach bursting out of their cocoon, my fingers moving frantically again as my eyes darted across her face looking for a smile, a curled lip, a roll of the eye, anything that would tell me what I should do next. Something was going to happen, Eric be damned. Our eyes locked. Even the faintest of sounds had stopped. Then she said, "You're so silly."

3. "IRON MAN" / *Black Sabbath* AND "WALK THIS WAY" / *Aerosmith and Run-D.M.C.*

Back in 1986, when I was ten, most of my classmates were trying to master their New Edition impersonations, rocking the latest pair of Pumas, shell-top Adidas, or Lee jeans. Meanwhile I was obsessed with how to get a growling-lion patch that had the name of my favorite band, Van Halen, leering out of the lion's pupils to put on my denim jacket. This jacket was usually offset by a pair of ghastly boots that I willingly scuffed up in an attempt to make them look like the buckle-laden hoofers that my heavy-metal heroes some-times wore. I occasionally accessorized these boots with a bandanna folded over in a diamond, which covered the area around my right ankle. And if it were not for my best friend at the time, Kiram, telling me that wearing tights or pasted-on jeans were not essential to proving oneself as a metalhead, I surely would have talked my mom out of buying my jeans a size or two too big so that I could don those as well.

I trusted Kiram's taste in heavy metal because he grew up listening to it. The information that Kiram shared with me came from what he'd learned from his older brother and sister.

Along with a shared interest in rock music, Kiram and I were both of Caribbean descent (he was from Guyana) and were both big wrestling fans. We especially enjoyed how these two spectacles were fused together by Hawk and Animal, the two members of the legendary tag team the Road Warriors who were stars during the heyday of the American and National Wrestling Associations.

Audiences didn't hate Hawk and Animal as much as they feared them. The two men disregarded the traditional wrestling plotline where the underdog gets a moment to shine before being toppled. Instead they barreled into the ring and commenced pummeling their opponents, sometimes even pinning their victims before their theme song, Black Sabbath's "Iron Man," finished playing. On countless other occasions their opponents either quit before the matches began or had to be coaxed back into the ring.

Who could blame their opponents? Hawk's and Animal's football-player physiques and their menacing tagline—"We snack on danger! We dine on death! And dead men don't make money!"—was more than enough to petrify their adversaries. This fear was amplified by the face paint that alternated between the hieroglyphics found on the faces of Maori warriors to the artwork emblazoned on disciples of the metal band Kiss.

It was exhilarating watching the ring shake as Hawk and Animal jumped up and down in their corner, further goading the crowd's hysteria and robbing their opponents of their last vestiges of courage.

Whenever I heard the first guitar chords of "Iron Man," a song featured on Black Sabbath's 1970 release *Paranoid*, goose bumps coursed all over my body. If I was in another room, I made a beeline to the TV to ensure I didn't miss any of the action. A Road Warriors match was like a building demolition, and the pulsating bass line of "Iron Man" was the explosion chosen to detonate the building, just as it incited wrestling audiences to hysteria.

As the Road Warriors barreled down the aisle, "Iron Man" ignited a rush of adrenaline through my body that felt as powerful as one of the duo's body slams. My head began tipping back and forth off its axis, sometimes almost taking my body with it as I tried playing the most intense, chubby Haitian virtuoso, Nikki Sixx–clone air guitar imaginable. While Ozzy ran through the lead vocals, I backed him up from in front of the TV: "I AM IRON MAN!"

Because of the Road Warriors I always associate "Iron Man" with an unrelenting rampage. At that time I desperately wanted to be the person leading the march, like Hawk and Animal, instead of the person having to retreat. I generally felt as if I was being reined in by my parents and teachers while others got a chance to do what they wanted, and even worse, got to do what they wanted to do to me. So the thought of being able to exact my will on the rest of the world was extremely alluring. I didn't want to kill anyone— I was merely captivated that somehow I could go from being the soft chubby kid to the strong "Iron Man."

I desperately wanted my opponents—the kids teasing me because of my accent or the way I dressed, and the teachers who seemed to take everyone else's side but mine—to fear me and clear out of my way. Still, I couldn't fight these battles alone and would need a tag-team partner of my own to watch my back, similar to the way Hawk protected Animal and vice versa—which is where Kiram came in.

Kiram walked through our hood with his head held high, ready to flip anyone the finger or just spit out "fuck you" as if he didn't already convey that in so many other ways. I, on the other hand, usually trailed behind him, smiling, fending off the accusations that I was trying to be a white boy by idolizing heavy-metal artists. "Don't you know where you came from? Don't you know what white people did to us?" the other black kids from school would ask—and as always, my answer was, "Yes, but . . ."*

I tried vehemently to explain to the other kids that I was a fan of Black Sabbath, Mötley Crüe, or Van Halen for the same reason that they loved DeBarge or New Edition. I was drawn to these rockers by the power they held over their adoring fans and the girls who practically fainted at the sight of them, just like the girls in our class went crazy at the mere mention of Ralph, Bobby, Ronnie, Ricky, and Mike. New Edition had the same black faces as me, but I felt closer to the white boys in Van Halen because they acted as if they

---

* Interestingly enough, many of the black kids in our class, myself included, revered the Junkyard Dog almost as much as they loved his theme song, none other than Queen's "Another One Bites the Dust." Little did we know—except Kiram, of course—that the song that we all admired was sung by an all-white band that was led by one of the most flamboyant front men of all time, Freddie Mercury.

didn't fit in, just like heavy metal or anything other than pop, R&B, reggae, and rap didn't fit in on our block. Having realized that no matter how much time I spent in front of the mirror practicing the dance moves of New Edition or Michael Jackson I wouldn't ever be able to walk in their shoes, I tried as valiantly as I could to learn to walk in my own.

Then one day, while watching the Saturday broadcast of a local music video show whose name I have long forgotten, everything changed. I had made a point of always watching this show because it often featured Van Halen's "Jump" video. They didn't play "Jump," but another song which practically made me forget about the group altogether.

I was watching the video of the groundbreaking Aerosmith and Run-D.M.C. collaboration "Walk This Way." I was confused at first because even though the tag for the video listed Run-D.M.C. as performers, the first group playing on-screen was Aerosmith, whose Joe Perry seemed to be tuning up his guitar before a jam session in a cleared-out garage. And on the other side of the garage wall was the rap group Run-D.M.C., who were trying to have their own studio session.

The layout in the two rooms couldn't have been any more different. On the Aerosmith side are the band's two most famous members: vocalist Steven Tyler and Perry. Perry is calmly stringing his guitar as Tyler flamboyantly gallivants with the microphone at the front of the room. Their room is slightly haggard, with water bottles littered throughout and a few posters hanging on an otherwise bare wall.

On the other side of the wall is Run-D.M.C.: emcees Darryl "D.M.C." McDaniels and Joseph "Run" Simmons, and deejay Jason "Jam Master Jay" Mizell. Absent from their side of the room are the instruments accompanying the Aerosmith artists. Their sound is fueled by Jam Master Jay's turntables and the amps and speakers which the turntables and the emcees' mics are plugged in to. Their side of the wall is branded with the group's trademark logo—a black background with the words Run-D.M.C. emblazoned in bold white block lettering.

Each time that Perry begins stroking his guitar and drawing out the melody from the original Aerosmith version of "Walk This Way," Jam Master Jay's scratching of his updated version of this same tune from the other side of the wall starts to overrule him. Perry, whose hard-driving guitar sound is laden with blues and folk riffs, was the driving force behind many of Aerosmith's recordings and the model for legions of later rock-and-roll guitarists. Similarly, Jam Master Jay became the godfather of rap deejays as he distinguished himself from other pioneers like Kool DJ Herc, Grandmaster Flash, and Cut Creator by revolutionizing the scratching techniques and seamlessly weaving in samples from rock and funk into the sets he arranged for Run-D.M.C. Jay sounds intent on proving to Perry that not only has he replicated Perry's guitar chords from the original "Walk This Way" recording but he has updated them with his improvisational scratching. The interplay between Perry and Jam Master Jay effectively brings these two groups together, transforming what at first sounds like two disparate musical genres into a synchronized fusion of sound and passion.

I wasn't even born when Aerosmith released the original "Walk This Way" in 1975, and were it not for Kiram telling me about it, I'm not sure how long it would have taken me to discover its existence. The song appeared on the album *Toys in the Attic*, which many consider to be the group's defining record. Aerosmith's version of "Walk This Way" sounds surprisingly mellower than the Run-D.M.C. version. Tyler speeds through his vocals, keeping pace with bassist Tom Hamilton rather than matching the grittiness of Perry's guitar chords. Run-D.M.C.'s version, which appears on their 1986 album *Raising Hell*, is far grittier than the original. Since Run and D.M.C. both have coarser edges to their voices, their vocals are more in line with the track being provided by Perry and Jam Master Jay.

As the "Walk This Way" video progressed I rocketed up from where I had been lying on the floor and into a new stratosphere of movement. For the first time that I could remember my body felt like it belonged to me. Dancing to "Walk This Way" I felt less like a chubby Haitian kid ambling across the worn-out green carpet of his parents' room, and more like a man exuding the same swagger shown by the men performing on the TV screen.

These perceived changes were affirmed that Monday in school. For the first time ever I felt as if I knew what everyone was talking about. They weren't talking about some party that I wasn't invited to, or some underground cut that an older brother or cousin had put them on to and which had yet to make its way aboveground to me. Everyone was talking about the "Walk This Way" video; and not only was everyone talking about it but they were talking about it to me.

They presumed that since I liked heavy metal I knew everything about each and every rock band. I remember being peppered with questions about Aerosmith: "Who are they?" "Do they like black people?" "Do they have any other songs like this?"

In an instant all the obscure information that I had culled from those metal magazines, which only a week earlier the same kids were teasing me for reading, was suddenly in high demand. I rattled off previous songs Aerosmith had performed, current information on the band, and encouraged them to check out the band's original version of "Walk This Way." It was bizarre because although Kiram knew much more about Aerosmith than I did, the black kids weren't concerned with his thoughts or his information, especially once he denounced Aerosmith by saying that their time had passed and that the real rockers to look out for were his beloved Mötley Crüe.

Having been everything from the kid who didn't speak English to the bully, and being on the verge of settling into the role of the weird black kid, I couldn't help but relish my newfound popularity, and was quite grateful to Aerosmith and Run-D.M.C.

Kiram, who had older siblings and had known most of the kids at our school since preschool, couldn't understand my need to fit in. Our relationship became slightly strained. He couldn't understand that the other kids had given him a pass to be what he wanted to be because he was Guyanese— a pass that I was never afforded as a nappy-haired black kid who seemed to deify long-haired white guys. When he went home he had a brother and sister to swap stories with about music, finding within his own home affirmation of his tastes. I, on the other hand, went home to parents who feared that I might be worshipping the devil and friends who, like my classmates, thought I wasn't black enough because I listened to heavy metal.

"Walk This Way" changed all of this because while my clothes and musical tastes hadn't changed, Run-D.M.C. had validated Aerosmith, virtually giving heavy metal a probationary ghetto pass. That meant I received one too. A space had finally opened up for me to be myself and be black, and this was an opportunity that I could not pass up. I gladly welcomed the chance to be the school's minister of heavy-metal information, dispensing random heavy-metal fact after random heavy-metal fact.

It was a trip experiencing this transition. The blacker I became the whiter Kiram seemed to become. Within a year we went from being brothers in arms to good friends trying to limn out our places in the world. The irony is that the distance between Kiram and I was partly brought about by Aerosmith and Run-D.M.C. breaking down the walls between rock and rap.

"Walk This Way" remains one of the influential songs in my life. When a wall fell down in a video, I went from being a walking contradiction, a big black Haitian kid who idolized hairy white boys, to simply being a young man who no longer needed an iron cask to feel confident in his own skin.

4. "TWICE MY AGE" / *Shabba Ranks and Krystal* **AND** "SORRY" / *Foxy Brown*

There was this guy in my seventh-grade class, Elijah, who had a way with the ladies. I eventually learned this was another way of saying he had a lot of problems with the ladies. Girls and guys alike thought Elijah was cool because he was two years older, had a full goatee, and looked like an East Indian Johnny Depp with a Trinidadian accent spiced with a tinge of New York flavor. He sounded a bit like Depp in *Pirates of the Caribbean*, minus the long hair and *some* of the drunken flightiness, but with all of the flirtatiousness. Elijah's *Black Pearl* was his cousin's Toyota Supra. While the rest of us trekked to I.S. 238 on buses or hoofed it if we lived closer, Elijah rolled up in the Supra with the music up and the windows down. Driving this car to school didn't make Elijah cooler in our eyes. It completely obliterated the cool scale.

As I said, Elijah had a way with the ladies, and when we were in the seventh grade he was dating two of the cutest girls in our grade. Debra was Indo-Guyanese and Sarah was Trinidadian. Messing around with Debra and Sarah incited bouts of truancy from Elijah. Since he couldn't be seen walking to or from school with either of them, he decided to skip class altogether or arrive an hour or so late. Elijah's plan was working smoothly until one day when he mixed them up over the phone, accidentally calling Debra "Sarah," after clicking over from a conversation with Sarah.

The next day Elijah came to school early and huddled a few of the guys from our class to help him devise a way to get out of this mess. He asked me to help revise the letter he had written for Debra and asked our opinion on when might be the best time to give her the mix tape that he recorded for her, which was anchored by the Foxy Brown reggae hit "Sorry." As Elijah appealed for our help, we teased him about his predicament until his face turned rust orange with anger. Daniel made one last dig before we adjourned to our various duties for this mission: "Did you put 'Twice My Age' on it too?"

As the Shabba Ranks and Krystal dancehall collaboration "Twice My Age" grew in popularity, so did the frequency of our jokes about Elijah's "old man" stature in school. Daniel, like most of us, knew Debra and Sarah from elementary school. He was particularly bold and sang the chorus whenever he spotted one of the girls in the hallway. Even though they hated admitting it, "Twice My Age" became synonymous with their love triangle, and Debra, Sarah, and Elijah eventually embraced the song and the ribbing it inspired.

Back in 1989 Shabba Ranks was well on his way to becoming dancehall's first international superstar. He had garnered plenty of fame in Jamaica and cities with significant West Indian populations like London, Miami, and New York with his "Wicked in Bed," "X-Rated," and "Love Punnany Bad." These hits were landmarks in the strain of dancehall called "slackness" that Ranks helped popularize. True to any slackness toast, these hits were explicit in their discussions of sex, yet still creative and witty enough to make them endearing. "Love Punnany Bad," where Shabba chants in his familiar gruff baritone about an almost childlike love of punnany, as if he's talking about loving cookies, is one of the best examples.

"Twice My Age," however, diverges from his slackness riddims and exhibits some of the other qualities that made Shabba famous in the late '80s and early '90s. During that period he was a master collaborator, partnering with artists ranging from the lesser-known ingenue Krystal, whom he teams up with on "Twice My Age," to more popular American artists like KRS-One, Johnny Gill, and Queen Latifah. Unfortunately I always felt that Ranks's duets with American artists were a bit too calculated, geared toward scoring a big hit and making money for his new label, Epic; they failed to resonate with his early followers as strongly as his collaborations with other Jamaican artists. Still, his desire to broaden his audience wasn't all about money since it is clear from his later work that Shabba was genuinely interested in experimenting with various styles and intent on proving that he is not just about slackness.

Except for maybe Beenie Man and more recent superstar Sean Paul, few dancehall artists have matched Ranks's prowess in establishing a rapport with women. These artists have female followings rivaling that of reggae crooners Beres Hammond and Gregory Isaacs, whose ballads often evoke comparisons to American soul singers Marvin Gaye and Sam Cooke. Regardless of whether he's boasting about his lovemaking skills on "Wicked in Bed" or offering the more patrician chant of a reluctant, slightly ornery sugar daddy on "Twice My Age," Ranks keeps the same balance on the mic that makes for successful pillow talk: raw yet romantic, sexy yet sensible. For example, on "Twice My Age," Ranks's verses outlining why an older man can give the young chanteuse what she wants, in terms of both money and expert loving, is balanced out by his insinuation that these pleasures come at an expense for them both. She's passing up the more youthful and stronger men her age, and he risks losing his money and good sense in trying to give her all that she wants.

Few people remember that this song is part of Ranks's catalog because of how luminously Krystal, the female lead on the record, shines. Her sinuous vocals are reminiscent of '80s R&B artist Stephanie Mills, who scored many soul hits, among them "(You're Puttin') A Rush on Me" and "Something in the Way (You Make Me Feel)." Like Mills's, Krystal's voice has a sense of innocence that makes her performance as the young siren whose heartstrings are being plucked by an aging bachelor quite believable. Krystal's vocals are layered with the kind of veritas that makes the listener believe that she can't end this relationship. Though this man vexes her, he is also the man who protects her from the terrifying option of being alone. Krystal's predicament may not be rational but it surely is real.

Krystal's next series of verses features her explaining to the younger version of herself why the look of love given to them by these older men is only a masquerade. This older, more sagacious Krystal speaks at a slower pace in a tone reminiscent of Nancy Wilson's jazz sound on, for example, "This Mother's Daughter."

Shabba and Krystal sing over a sped-up drum machine snare rhythm with dollops of bass. The interplay between Shabba's voice and the beat on "Twice My Age" is sheer brilliance. Ranks's ability to scat alongside beats as if he was a ragamuffin Cab Calloway contributed to his general success and helped make "Twice My Age" more appealing. Before being lampooned on *In Living Color* and by African American comics like Cedric the Entertainer, Ranks's scatting ability was revered by listeners who recognized it as a facet of his musicianship, a distinct element of his toasting style, and not as these comics presented it: an unintelligible form of Jamaican patois.

"Twice My Age" is a creative musical production fusing reggae, dancehall, the blues, R&B, and jazz, which far outshines the quips launched at Elijah and his two love interests. Upon hearing the "Twice My Age" joke for the umpteenth time after recruiting our expertise to help him win back Debra, Elijah seemed serious when he shot back to Daniel, "That ain't funny yo." We were all ready to take him seriously until he burst out laughing.

It's actually unfortunate that we used this song in such a trifling way because it's one of my favorite songs of all time, an unadulterated favorite that reigns far above Elijah's misguided attempt to wield its powers.

"Sorry" is a song I've loved so much that I didn't take the time to find out who sang it until recently. I've just always enjoyed its presence in my life, knowing that it will be there as long as there are summertime picnics, West Indians waxing nostalgic over rounds of Red Stripe, and people looking to make amends for indiscretions in a relationship. Once I knew I was writing this book, though, I knew I had to find out who the performer was. After putting a call in to my friend DJ 4Sight, I got the name of the artist: Foxy Brown, formerly known as "that woman."

Brown's "Sorry" is in fact a cover of Tracy Chapman's "Baby Can I Hold You," from her 1988 debut album. In spite of her association with Chapman—whose first two albums, *Tracy Chapman* and *Crossroads* (1989), were commercial and critical successes—Brown's 1989 album, *Sorry*, didn't fare as well. However, if you were living in my neighborhood back in 1989 and heard "Sorry" piping out of the sound systems in the tricked-out Toyota Supras driven by the Guyanese and Trini cats, you would've been hardpressed to make an argument that Chapman was more popular than Brown.

In its arrangement, "Sorry" has none of the frills associated with '80s music. There are no eerie space- or horror-movie intrusions. Brown sings in what is practically a monotone, bypassing any of the octave gymnastics performed by divas like Whitney Houston, or the somber brooding lilts of an Anita Baker or Sade. Brown is neither perky nor seductive like Gloria Estefan and Janet Jackson, or even as spirited as Tracy Chapman on "Baby Can I Hold You," who seems far more exasperated by the indiscretion prompting the song and ready to confront her lover than Brown does. Brown sounds as if she's consoling her lover, conceding to still loving him at the song's outset, which immediately strips her voice of the cynicism that draws out the fire in Chapman's recording. Plus the tender bass line sailing under Brown's voice helps undo some of the hurt incited by her lover's indiscretion. "Sorry" feels more romantic than the lyrics actually intend it to be, which, along with Brown's West Indian lilt, helped advance its popularity in our neighborhood. It is also one of the reasons why Brown's version works well as a slow jam at many parties, a tune linked to the sight of couples locked in an embrace on the dance floor.

More than once I've caught myself watching a couple at a party, following them as they move side to side to the drum beat, the man tapping out the keyboard notes on the small of a woman's back, the woman tickling out the saxophones' flares on his shoulder blades. During these moments I try imagining scenarios where they might've put the song to use; maybe it was the time she caught him with one of her sorority sisters, or maybe it was just a few hours ago when one of them mixed up the time they were supposed to depart for the party. When I snap out of these moments, I find myself wondering why I'm not dancing with anyone or I'm transported back to the seventh grade, sitting around in a huddle with Elijah and some of the other guys as Elijah asks me to help him revise his letter.

Elijah took a risk by presenting Debra a mix tape anchored by "Sorry"; while its title may suggest otherwise, "Sorry" is not an apology. He may have paid little attention to the words. Then again, since he was the Trinidadian

Johnny Depp, I shouldn't have been surprised that Debra accepted an apology anyway, and once he agreed to break up with Sarah (or so she thought), they dated until the girls went on to high school. After a while we stopped seeing Elijah in class, and soon after that around the campus altogether, as he sailed further into a sea of truants.

5. "ME SO HORNY" / *2 Live Crew*

I was eleven years old when Stanley Kubrick's *Full Metal Jacket* first hit theaters. When I saw the promotions for the film, it appeared to be a redux of the 1986 Oliver Stone picture *Platoon*. My friends and I believed it wasn't worth spending money to see it in theaters when we could wait until it came out on video. We weren't only insulted that Hollywood would try to dupe us into paying for the same film twice (in full disclosure we didn't see *Platoon* in theaters either; it was the principle) but we couldn't understand the fascination with Vietnam.

There was talk in our social studies classes and during newscasts about the end of the war in Vietnam. For a spell, pristine images of President Ronald Reagan at the Arlington National Cemetery in Virginia and the unveiling of Maya Lin's Vietnam Veterans Memorial supplanted the images of Vietnam veterans that my friends and I were more accustomed to. We were used to seeing these former soldiers idling in front of the men's home near Parsons Boulevard in Queens or panhandling in the 169th Street train station. The vets were distinguishable from other men in similar circumstances by the military attire that they usually wore, shirts with nametags and stripes affixed to them and on occasion a jacket with a VFW or POW patch. These men often made bitter declarations about their time in Vietnam or the struggles that they were facing at home after the war.

These haggard-looking men were a far cry from the handsome actors whom my friend Samir and I saw in *Full Metal Jacket*. Samir and I laughed endlessly as they sought to make their way through basic training in the first half of the movie. We joked about which of these men we favored. Early in the film we decided that I was Private Gomer Pyle (Vincent D'Onofrio) and he was Private Joker (Matthew Modine). As the film wore on, we each adopted new identities. I inherited the role of the peace-loving, Nietzsche-quoting Private Joker, and Samir became the renegade Animal Mother (Adam Baldwin).

Our laughter ceased when one of the characters committed suicide by stuffing his rifle into his mouth and blowing his brains out on the evening of his graduation from boot camp—an act that eerily enough would be replicated almost to a tee by one of our friends, and another *Full Metal Jacket* devotee, two years later.* This sudden outburst of violence

---

*Our pal's death was actually reported as accidental, but my friends and I always found this claim to be rather dubious because it took place a few short days after his graduation from middle school, and we were skeptical that he was reckless enough with a gun to fatally shoot himself.

in the movie caught Samir and I off guard. If Kubrick's intent was to make the point that one should never get comfortable in a war zone, we had learned our lesson.

We were similarly caught off guard by the next scene. Just as the suicide in the dimly lit latrine was settling in, the setting swiftly shifted to a sun-drenched day in Da Nang. A tall Vietnamese woman gradually filled up the screen as her leggy frame strolled into view. The camera is focused on her butt, which is barely covered by the black leather miniskirt complementing her gold leather heels. As she walks up to the two American soldiers sitting at a table outside a café, Nancy Sinatra's 1966 hit "These Boots Are Made for Walkin'" plays in the background. Kubrick's decision to use the biggest hit by the daughter of Hollywood legend Frank Sinatra to introduce a prostitute speaks well of the dysfunctional libidos of Vietnam soldiers who fantasized about Ann-Margret as they fucked Vietnamese prostitutes.

Moments after shocking us with the suicide, Kubrick had us laughing again with the banter between the prostitute (Papillon Soo) and the two soldiers, Private Joker and Rafterman (Kevyn Major Howard).

"What the fuck did she just say? Yo, rewind that, son," Samir blurted out while pointing to the TV screen, doing revolutions with his hand as if he could rewind the tape through his gesturing.

After rewinding the scene about five or six times, Samir and I were now certain that the prostitute did indeed say, "Me so horny. Me love you long time."

Two years later when we heard the same line used as a hook on the 2 Live Crew song "Me So Horny," Samir and I discovered that we weren't the only two guys obsessed with that scene in *Full Metal Jacket*. Using the Da Nang prostitute's famous line as its refrain, the Miami foursome—consisting of Luther Campbell (Uncle Luke, Luke Skywalker), Chris Wong Won (Fresh Kid Ice), Mark Ross (Brother Marquis), and David Hobbs (Mr. Mixx)—scored a major hit with "Me So Horny," the lead track on their 1989 album *As Nasty as They Wanna Be*.

As Nasty as They Wanna Be was one of the most controversial albums of the late '80s and early '90s because of its explicit sexual lyrics. It became a lightning rod for politicians seeking to put restraints on a music industry that they thought was careening out of control. The political turmoil and accompanying media attention swirling around the album's release helped transform 2 Live Crew from a relatively obscure regional act into platinum-selling artists. Unfortunately for the group, exorbitant legal costs prohibited them from fully reaping the benefits of the commercial success of *As Nasty as They Wanna Be*.

It was also one of the most creative albums of the era. The album migrates from "The F--K Shop," a song driven by a new-wave beat, to the more raucous "Fraternity Record," one of the songs where 2 Live Crew practices their trademark call-and-response routine with their fans. As "Reggae Joint" reveals, these experiments are not always successful, but when they are, as in the case of "Me So Horny," they flourish.

Because of its explicit lyrics, "Me So Horny" initially drew a following through endorsements by club deejays and sporadic airplay on late-night and college radio programs by deejays who were either courageous enough to test FCC rules or creative enough to patch together a clean version before the group released one in late 1989. This underground quality to the song and the cartoonish lyrics left me unsure at first whether "Me So Horny" was an Al Yankovic–esque satire; a picaresque romp like the '90 break-out hit from Digital Underground, "The Humpty Dance"; or whether 2 Live Crew was seriously trying to establish themselves as rappers and introduce a new sound. In terms of flow, none of the members of the group was on the same level as any of the late '80s or early '90s heavyweights Big Daddy Kane, Ice Cube, or Rakim. They do compare favorably, however, to some of the individual talents in groups such as 3rd Bass, Kid 'n Play, and Cube's cohorts in N.W.A.

Of 2 Live Crew, Fresh Kid Ice is arguably the strongest rapper because of his witty puns and ability to maintain a consistent output throughout the album. He is part Paul Wall, the more contemporary cherubic Houston rapper who appears to be Ice's twin in terms of size and lyrical deport-ment, and part Too Short, the latter-day Bay Area rap icon known for his own sexually explicit lyrics. Ice, who along with Mr. Mixx was one of the founding members of the group when they were originally based in Oakland, also shares his Bay Area mate's penchant for the lyrically absurd:

> It's true you were a virgin until you met me
> I was the first to make you hot and wetty-wetty . . .

Yet, like Too Short, Ice knew that a rapper needed to be more than just explicit to keep the listener's attention. In his cadence, Ice cheerfully delivers a quarter-note flow similar to the one that distinguished Too Short from his peers. Ice often sounds as if he is ready to burst with glee over the fact that he is rhyming. He practically laughs at his puns before he finishes delivering them.

Brother Marquis, on the other hand, is the group's understated personality, though in the "Horny" video he's found walking around on all fours revealing his own knack for the absurd. While his rhymes are clever in spurts, they're short of memorable. Yet Marquis is a better rapper/lyricist than Uncle Luke, who's more of a hype man barking out orders to the audience than an actual lyricist. Luke has the same businesslike approach to rapping as the late Eazy-E had and that Diddy now exudes. None of them are lyricists, but all three managed to import their personalities onto the projects of the artists they worked with, such as N.W.A., Notorious B.I.G., and 2 Live Crew. As Uncle Luke went from being manager to front man to media lightning rod, 2 Live Crew went from being a Miami version of Digital Underground to the most notorious rap group this side of N.W.A. The fact that he doesn't even have a verse on "Me So Horny," yet is still inextricable from the song, is one testament to how much his personality outpaced his actual artistic contributions to the group's efforts.

Where the group really excels on "Me So Horny" is with Mr. Mixx's production. His mix of soundscapes is on par with some of the work of Dr. Dre, Eric B., or DJ E-Z Rock from that same period. Back in 1989 when New York–area producers like Marley Marl and Diamond D were refining their prowess for inserting funk- or jazz-inspired piano loops on their records, Mixx was in his lair mining porno movie clips, dance tracks, and electropop. These sound effects helped distinguish 2 Live Crew from their New York and California counterparts. Mixx's use of film sounds was a precursor to the RZA's creative interpolations of kung fu sound effects on the Wu-Tang Clan's albums.

These loops also marked an evolution from the nude drum machine and the turntable riffs found on many of the rap records from the early '80s. (Think of Jam Master Jay's work on the album *Run-D.M.C.*, for example.) On "Horny," Mixx proves that the capabilities of the drum machines and turntables had yet to be fully exhausted and that there was still a lot more amusement to be gleaned—all that you needed to do was turn up the bass.

However, you can't have a song or a whole genre of sound based on bass alone, and 2 Live Crew and their Miami bass peers, the 69 Boyz ("Tootsee Roll") and Quad City DJ's ("C'Mon N' Ride It [The Train]") were extremely adept at discovering hooks meant to remain in a listener's head long after its first hearing. A person may never remember a line uttered by any of the emcees from "Me So Horny," but it's doubtful you'll be able to get the refrain out of your head shortly after hearing the song. Even for a musical genre where artists are forever throwing grammar, spelling, and syntax by the wayside, the declaration "Me so horny" distinguishes itself. The phrase isn't invented; it's organic immigrant English and not the layered jargon espoused by certain rappers. Think of Jay-Z's "IZZO (Hova)," for example. An excellent song, but trying to decipher what "Fo' shizzle my nizzle used to dribble down in VA" means doesn't really compare to the tantalizing experience of opening your ears to something different yet strangely familiar.

Unlike their East and West Coast peers who were on the verge of becoming embroiled in an epic battle, 2 Live Crew and their Florida colleagues were interested in making party music, music that people could shake their asses to, not music that people (especially guys) stand around nodding their heads to, or try to rap along with in vain attempts at matching their favorite emcees word for word. The depth of the lyrics on "Me So Horny" cannot compare to Rakim's mastery on "I Know You Got Soul," but the way in which the song is structured to make the call-and-response sequence an innate aspect rather than the whim of a hype man makes it easier to dance to.

Their lack of depth and lyrical gymnastics has played a great part in 2 Live Crew's banishment from the golden age of hip-hop lore, a development which undermines the remarkable impact that they had in the music industry and in shaping the course of rap music. They redefined the high stakes of publicity and what's constituted as misogynistic and obscene in rap music, reinvigorated a discussion of censorship in America, and somehow implicated or attracted the attention of every sector of American society to their cause.*

*Music enthusiasts, and heavy-metal fans in particular, will remember that the controversy surrounding 2 Live Crew took place four years after the 1985 Senate hearings initiated by the Parents Music Resource Center (PMRC), which was chaired by Tipper Gore. At these hearings rockers Frank Zappa and Dee Snider teamed up with folksinger John Denver to counter the PMRC's attack against heavy metal, which the PMRC saw as the culprit spurring rape, teen pregnancy, and suicide. The PMRC did not win all-out censorship, but they did convince record companies to put parental advisory labels on tapes and CDs with explicit content. These labels were for a time referred to as the "Tipper Sticker."

Long before I knew of his work as a literary theorist and chair of Harvard's African American Studies Department, I had heard of Henry Louis Gates Jr. because of his testimony on behalf of 2 Live Crew. That someone who would later become a Harvard professor would testify on their behalf speaks volumes to the magnitude of the events in which 2 Live Crew was implicated. Gates also defended the group in a *New York Times* article that refuted the claims of *Newsweek* columnist George Will, a debate later explored by law professor Kimberle Crenshaw, among others.

As Crenshaw alluded to in her article about the case, 2 Live Crew's trial was also a good example of the complicated nature of the enduring struggle between the message and the beat in rap music. During 2 Live Crew's trial, black female rap enthusiasts and their male allies were expected to suppress their critiques and support the group in their alleged crusade against unfair prosecution. Misogyny took a backseat to the never-ending struggles of black men against the nation's justice system. Little did it seem to matter that it was a troupe of black men who were producing the misogynist material.

Are the lyrics on many of the songs on *As Nasty as They Wanna Be*, including "Me So Horny," obscene, misogynist, and offensive to women? Yes. However, when I was fourteen in 1990, I was on the side arguing that 2 Live Crew's music was no less offensive or gratuitous than the Hollywood movies from which they drew their inspiration. I often agreed with friends that "Me So Horny" posed no less of a threat to anyone than *Full Metal Jacket* did—thought if I had thought more closely about my friend's suicide at that point I might have reconsidered that opinion. But since I didn't, I kept right on dancing to "Me So Horny."

Regardless of what I thought, I barely understood what was going on. The extensive media coverage made it hard to discern when the reel show had ended and the real court proceedings were occurring.* I remember sitting in my parents' living room with Samir and watching the news segment about 2 Live Crew's arrest for obscenity and wondering whether this was a crude joke. Uncle Luther comported himself as if he was born to be in front of the camera, casting himself as a modern-day picaro or the Dr. Ruth of hip-hop, as he once called himself. Luke was alluding to the sex expert who he felt was lauded for discussing the same issue—sex—that he and his bandmates were under attack for rapping about. One minute Uncle Luke was depicted being arrested and the next he was on a news show discussing how this trial was un-American and saying that 2 Live Crew was being unfairly censored.

It's interesting to note that after 2 Live Crew was acquitted of the charges leveled against them for their Florida performance, the same aggressive posturing that they used for their sex-laden exploits, and which they were later caricatured for, were adopted by rappers seeking to verify their street credentials on wax. Any intervention that one might have imagined occurring with the release of anti-violence anthems "Self Destruction" and "We're All in the Same Gang" was abandoned as the rap industry lusted after profits, using the same provocateur marketing strate-

*A shout-out goes to bell hooks and Grand Puba for turning a young man's witty turn of phrase "reel to real" into something meaningful.

gies that almost left 2 Live Crew bankrupt. Today the group's influence is visible in the sounds and antics of artists like Lil Jon and the Eastside Boyz and the Ying Yang Twins.

Fifteen years later, and without the sentimental blinders of a fourteen-year-old boy to shape my opinions, I am still wrestling with the same questions posed by the release of 2 Live Crew's controversial songs "Me So Horny" and "Pop That P Ussy." The latest song to ignite this inner turmoil was the Ying Yang Twins' "Wait (The Whisper Song)." While walking down Washington Avenue in Brooklyn, I spotted a group of children surrounding a car blasting the unedited version of "Wait (The Whisper Song)." "How can you let your kids listen to that shit?" I wondered aloud to the friend walking with me.

Have I become an adult or a hypocrite? I ask myself this question because while I'd be damned if I'd let my kids (if I had any) within earshot of that song, I don't have any problem with a deejay bumping it in the club. Sure the lyrics are weak, but that beat is sick, which was the same issue that I faced with "Me So Horny." Still acknowledging that dichotomy and accepting dope beats if they're not affiliated with equally moving lyrics is a sign of how far away I am from deciding once and for all whether to continue supporting these types of records with my dollars and my dancing, or to fight to eradicate them from our society.

It's been a surreal experience meditating on "Me So Horny." Prior to sitting down to write *Songs in the Key of My Life,* the only other encounters I had with the song was at strip clubs. It was nowhere to be found in my CD or MP3 collection, much less my mind. Once I started writing, thoughts of *Full Metal Jacket*, my friend's death, and academics defending potty-mouth rappers took hold of my imagination. "Me So Horny" became a most unlikely muse, arresting my thoughts and deeply challenging my notions of who I am today by pitting me against who I was back then. This book is as much about what I have to say about songs as it is about what these songs have to say about me.

6. "STAR-SPANGLED BANNER" /
performed by Whitney Houston

It was Super Bowl Sunday, January 1991. Like most football fans, I went through that day in eager anticipation of the evening's tilt between the New York Giants and the Buffalo Bills. I was fourteen and fondly remembered the Giants' victory over the Denver Broncos in Super Bowl XXI four years earlier. While I looked forward to another Giants' win that night in Tampa, I had mixed feelings about which team to root for since the Giants were playing another team from the state of New York. Joining me for that night's game was my friend Tim, with whom I had watched practically all the Jets and Giants games leading up to the Super Bowl.

As Tim and I cleared off my parents' coffee table for the food we'd purchased to eat while watching the Super Bowl, we were more focused on figuring out how much rum we'd be able to slip into our Cokes without my dad noticing than any of the pregame activities occurring on-screen. This was the second time that Tim and I were watching a Super Bowl together. We outdid the preparations of our inaugural gathering by having a surplus of potato chips, candy, and even a pizza on hand for this viewing. We also exiled my brother to Tim's apartment next door where he could watch cartoons with Tim's sisters. Tim and I wanted to have a true "man's" Super Bowl party and looked forward to the arrival of the friends we had invited over.

The last thing on our minds was the national anthem. Back then, you couldn't pay us enough to watch the singing of the "Star-Spangled Banner." Those three minutes before a broadcast sporting event were better served making that last run to the bathroom or to the corner bodega to get some snacks. However, since we already had all the food we needed and each was into about his third pizza slice, neither of us was going anywhere, lest we give the other person an opportunity to sneak in an extra slice. Tim and I at least conceded to respecting the moment of silence for the soldiers fighting in the first Gulf War because we had friends engaged in that conflict.

Little did we know that as we prepared to watch Super Bowl XXV that the evening's most outstanding performance wouldn't be delivered by any of the Herculean athletes we eagerly looked forward to seeing play. Instead, the night belonged to a chanteuse light enough for most of these men to pick up as effortlessly as they do a football.

When Whitney Houston's performance began, Tim and I were immediately captivated. Houston was wearing a white jumpsuit with stars-and-stripes piping running along the side and the front of her jacket. She had her hair pulled back by a white headband, which completed an outfit that made her look like she was there to watch the game more than anything else. Once she started singing, though, it was obvious that she was actually there to steal the show.

I halted my offensive on the pizza slice in my hand and looked over at Tim, who had also stopped scarfing down his slice. We lowered our plates to the coffee table in front of us and gave Houston our undivided attention. Our immature levity sailed out the door as she scaled another octave on the anthem's register.

Having never seen Marvin Gaye's performance before the 1984 NBA All-Star Game, itself a memorable performance from what I've heard, I rank Houston's as the greatest I've ever seen. Singing live in front of more than seventy thousand people, Houston managed to hit each note and enunciate every word as if she were alone in her studio rehearsing. While each line offered her an opportunity to reveal her mortality to the billion people watching all over the world, she didn't compromise the integrity of her performance by skirting any of the high notes that the anthem called for.

I was watching a different Whitney. Her jumpsuit was a stark contrast to the sequined gowns I was used to seeing her sport. In spite of her enormous success as an artist and long list of hits, I always associated Houston with her sentimental ballad "Greatest Love of All," a song which Tim and I enjoyed singing out of key whenever Houston appeared on-screen, regardless of whether or not she was singing it. We especially enjoyed singing the opening lines— "I believe that children are the future, teach them well and let them lead the way"—in an exaggerated falsetto. But on this night, Tim and I sat completely still, shut up, and let an angel sing.

The game itself wasn't bad. Both teams relied on their all-pro running backs to barrel over defenders for each available yard—not the most aesthetically pleasing game to watch. But it did feature one of the greatest endings in Super Bowl history, a last-second field goal attempt by Buffalo kicker Scott Norwood. Norwood missed the field goal, thereby denying Buffalo a chance for at least one victory in their run of four consecutive trips to the Bowl. The next morning all of the news reports focused on the two legends erected the previous night in Tampa. One, Norwood, became the face for another of sport's legendary missed opportunities at greatness. Even though he lasted one more season with the Bills and was the team's all-time leading scorer, he was never able to escape the scrutiny of that missed kick.

The other legend was Houston. For many people her rendition of the anthem represented a grand homage to the soldiers who fought in the Gulf War. This in spite of the fact that, as was later disclosed, it was a prerecorded performance. We'd been captivated by the illusion. Her Super Bowl rendition of the "Star-Spangled Banner" turned into a top-twenty hit in 1991, and a decade later, after the September 11 attacks on the World Trade Center, a charity rerelease of this selection raised more than one million dollars for 9/11 victims.

Hollywood producers wanted to see if Houston could be a box-office draw as well. She was. The Bills continued losing Super Bowls and Houston released three hit movies—*The Bodyguard* (1992), *Waiting to Exhale* (1995), and *The*

Preacher's Wife (1996)—each of which was accompanied by a platinum-selling soundtrack anchored by a Houston single. In a five-year span, she made the transition from successful recording artist to box-office draw with an ease rarely exhibited by any artist, much less a black female artist, a fact that anyone who saw Mariah Carey's film *Glitter* can attest to.

I can't believe that it's already been fifteen years since that night. I am amazed that the United States is still engaged in a war in the Persian Gulf. Equally unbelievable is what has become of Houston's career. A decade ago, she was helping revolutionize the story of Cinderella by headlining an all-star production that featured a multiracial cast, including Houston protégée singer/actress Brandy Norwood as Cinderella. A few years later, in December 2002, Houston was profiled in the media as someone with increasingly erratic behavior. During an interview with Diane Sawyer about her alleged drug addiction, Houston bizarrely replied, "Crack is cheap. I make too much money to use crack. Crack is wack." Three years later her career took another downturn when she co-starred in a reality show starring her husband, fellow singer Bobby Brown.

The massive scrutiny under which Houston has tried conducting a personal life, causing her to fight off allegations of everything from drug abuse to an unhappy marriage, appears to be having an impact on her voice. During one recent award-show performance, I was saddened by her inability to ascend heights on the scale that she once climbed so gracefully. Her always lithe body now seemed gaunt as she brought out her daughter, Bobbi Kristina, to stand alongside her. After she finished singing, she stood onstage hugging her daughter, who looked as shaken by what had just transpired as those in attendance. The rest of the world may have taken another step in losing a legend that night, but the girl onstage was wrestling with something much more profound—losing her mother.

There's time for Houston to turn her life around and receive help to overcome her issues. In fact, there will always be time for someone as talented as Houston. She showed everyone that night during Super Bowl XXV that when she sings, time has a strange way of standing still.

7. "CROSSROAD" / *Bone Thugs-N-Harmony*

When my brother was in the seventh grade, Randy and I had established a routine where we'd go to the park in the mornings and play basketball with friends. While I was at work in the afternoons, he'd go over to his girlfriend Toni's neighborhood in South Jamaica to hang out. On days that my mom was home, he'd tell her that he was going to visit his friend "Dan's block." He wasn't totally lying—Toni did live on Dan's block—but Randy stretched the truth because our mom thought that at thirteen years old he was too young to have a girlfriend.

Randy covered this relationship well. He always made sure to return to our neighborhood before nightfall. It was like clockwork. As the sun gave way to twilight every summer evening, I'd see a silhouette of Randy making his way up from Jamaica Avenue. He'd give me and my friends who were hanging out in front of our building a nod as if to say, "What's up," go inside the apartment, wash the dishes, take a shower, and if the spirit moved him come back outside to hang with us. Randy's regimen mirrored the one that I had established with our parents when I was his age, where regardless of where I was in the city, I found a way to be back inside our apartment at 11:10 P.M.

Randy's schedule was tragically disturbed when a few weeks into his summer vacation several members of Toni's family were murdered in their Queens home. Reports of these murders were the staple of evening news and front pages of the city's newspapers until the next tragedy or scandal came along. While I was deeply shaken by these accounts, Mom had no idea that Randy was intimately connected to one of the surviving members of that family. Thoughts about all the evenings that Randy had spent hanging out with Toni in her neighborhood stifled my ability to think about her dead family members. I sweated over what could have happened if the assailants had arrived earlier and Randy was still there. How would I have explained his death and my knowledge of his clandestine rendezvouses with Toni to our parents? I couldn't mull over these scenarios for too long because having previously taken the responsibility of keeping his secret from our parents, it was now my responsibility to help steer him through his mourning. I made myself available for conversations after he attended vigils at Toni's house and consoled him when, fearing for her safety, Toni's relatives sent her to live with family members outside of New York.

This was my first encounter with death where I had to do the consoling. I did my best to replicate my father's actions

from when my maternal grandmother died four years earlier. He spent hours by my mother's side, saying nothing.
He relieved her of any household duties and then quickly
stepped aside when it became clear that she needed the sta-
bility that these tasks provided. Similarly, I sat there with
Randy on his bed watching him pore over newspaper clippings of the murders. When he talked, I listened. When
friends who didn't know what Randy was coping with tried
prodding him into laughter, or asked, "What's wrong with
him?" I never let them go too far.

Finally, when it seemed as if he was ready, I started asking him some of the questions that I had been longing to
ask: "Were you ever in danger hanging out at her house?"
"Why were they murdered?" The hardest question for us to
brook was also the simplest one: "How do you feel?" We
both knew that "I'm aiight, I'm maintainin," or "I'm cool"
wouldn't be enough.

One day I walked in on him as he sat in our room looking at one of the newspaper clippings. It was the middle of
the afternoon and the little bit of natural light that came
into the room had already been eclipsed by the red house
outside our window. I asked him, "What are you up to?"

Without taking his eyes off the clipping, Randy offered,
"I still don't believe it. I was just over by her house and saw
her cousins coming in as I was leaving." He paused.

"Did you know them well?" I asked and took a seat next
to him.

"Nah. I used to see 'em around her house and said 'what's
up' to them, but I didn't really know 'em." He was shaking
his head. "But it still hurts you know, because I know
Toni."

That was the first time I heard him say that it hurt. Taking the clipping out of his hand, I prepared to tell him something to the effect of "Don't worry. I'm here to help in whatever way I can," when Randy mentioned the Bone Thugs-N-Harmony song "Crossroad." It seems that someone was wearing a T-shirt at one of the vigils that said SEE YOU AT THE CROSSROADS. Randy's reference to Bone Thugs-N-Harmony stuck with me at first because I was surprised to hear about people wearing T-shirts to funerals. I was raised to think that funerals were formal occasions where you dressed as conservatively as you would for a wedding. And of all groups for people to draw inspiration from, why Bone Thugs-N-Harmony?

I first remember hearing them through the single off of *E 1999 Eternal,* "1st of Tha Month." Partially fueled by my lack of appreciation for the accelerated speed at which they rhyme, my initial impression was that the track was trite and yet another example of a rap group lampooning the plight of poor people. I missed the bluesy-lyrical elements of "1st of Tha Month," characterized by the group's ability to speak authoritatively on a grave topic—being on welfare—without dampening the spirits of their audience.

Despite rap blossoming into an international phenomenon, I was still biased against any rap acts that weren't from New York. If a rapper hailed from elsewhere, I needed to be convinced that they were not a contrived commercial gimmick before I even considered taking them seriously, much less purchasing their music. Bone Thugs-N-Harmony's fast-paced flows and Midwestern origins were just the types of devices that I thought record companies would use to market artists lacking any real talent. However, when I heard "Crossroad," my reservations about Bone Thugs-N-Harmony's talent, along with whatever remaining doubts I had about their intentions as artists, slowly receded. This process was eventually completed when I saw the video of the song.

"Crossroad" did not enthrall me merely because it features rappers speaking eloquently about death. Pete Rock and C.L. Smooth had already managed this feat in 1992 with "They Reminisce over You (T.R.O.Y.)," the moving tribute to their close friend and former member of Heavy D and the Boyz, Troy Dixon. Propelled by Pete Rock's trademark horn loops and C.L. Smooth's conscientious rhymes, "They Reminisce over You (T.R.O.Y.)" was the first rap song on which I'd heard a rapper offer a personal account of the impact of a loved one's death on his life. It distinguished itself from earlier anthems like "Self Destruction" and "We're All in the Same Gang" because it was an individual's recounting of the meaning of life and not a group effort in which stopping senseless violence was the focus. Pete Rock's mix of horn loops, cymbals, and strings of synthesized bass and keyboard superlatively complement C.L. Smooth's verses. "They Reminisce over You (T.R.O.Y.)" is an example of jazz and hip-hop meeting on the other side of the Marvin Gaye highway, inspired by the conscientious musicianship and sensitive lyricism prevalent in the work of Gaye and many of his peers from the '60s and '70s.

Likewise, the Geto Boys (Scarface, Willie D., and Bushwick Bill) rode this highway to Hayes Junction, aptly named after Memphis legend Isaac Hayes. In his heyday Hayes's somber arrangements were used to amplify the harrowing experiences of other vocalists, blaxploitation films, and, on occasion, his own vocals. Rhyming over a solemn track reminiscent of Hayes's classic "By the Time I Get to Phoenix," the Geto Boys present what Bushwick Bill described on *Yo MTV Raps* as three psychological profiles: "a paranoid hustler, a manic depressive individual and a schizophrenic Bushwick" on their 1991 single "Mind Playing Tricks on Me." Unlike Pete Rock and C.L. Smooth, who characterize death as part of life's cycle, the Geto Boys envision it as a nightmarish figure stalking the three people described by Bushwick Bill. "Mind Playing Tricks on Me" was a departure from the jazz and James Brown funk-inspired melodies of New York rappers as well as the Parliament/Funkadelic reincarnate g funk promoted by West Coast rappers on their gritty gangsta tracks.

In their video "Tha Crossroads," Bone Thugs-N-Harmony resurrects the image of the demonic figure stalking his prey first seen in the "Mind Playing Tricks on Me" video. Just as in the Geto Boys video, Bone Thugs-N-Harmony's grim reaper is a black man draped in an all-black outfit topped off with a black hat. This figure is not the devil incarnate as some might infer but more likely an adaptation of the voodoo icon Baron Samedi, whom a Wikipedia editor defines as a figure who "stands at the *crossroads* where the souls of dead humans pass on their way to" the next world, or when "spirits cross over into our world." Baron Samedi is also usually depicted decked in all black, just like the figure looming over the souls in the Geto Boys and Bone Thugs-N-Harmony videos, an image punctuated by these memorable lines from Scarface's verse on "Mind Playing Tricks on Me":

He owns a black hat like I own
A black suit and a cane like my own . . .

If this connection to Baron Samedi was intentional, then "Mind Playing Tricks on Me" director Richard Hunt provided "Tha Crossroads" director Michael Martin with a rich archetype to use as the foundation for the Bone Thugs-N-Harmony video. Picking up where Hunt left off, Martin replaces his predecessor's bare-bones camera work and plain settings with glossier imagery and special effects. And where in the "Mind Playing Tricks on Me" video the focus is on the trio's paranoia, in the "Tha Crossroads" video the Baron Samedi figure is actually depicted snatching the lives of Bone Thugs-N-Harmony's friends and family members. "Tha Crossroads" climaxes with a powerful scene of the Baron Samedi figure leading the cavalcade of lives he's snatched up to a mountaintop while holding a baby, the last life he's seen taking in the video, in his arm. At this point in the video, the Samedi figure has discarded his hat and coat and has been outfitted with a pair of angel wings. Making the procession that more striking is the hologram of Bone Thugs-N-Harmony mentor Eazy-E that appears as they are walking up the mountainside and again when they reach the mountaintop. Eazy-E, who was also a founding member of N.W.A., had died in March of that year and "Tha Crossroads" became a tribute to him.

"Crossroad" frames the harmonizing of Bone Thugs-N-Harmony in a different light than their first single, "1st of Tha Month," does. The fast-paced cadence that I once saw as a nuisance is so resplendent on "Crossroad" that the echoes reverberating from Bone Thugs-N-Harmony's lyrics evoke another sound unto itself, another level of rhythm. Thus, instead of coming across as tormented figures like their predecessors the Geto Boys, Bone Thugs-N-Harmony sounds like part youth choir, part urban griots, and part twenty-third-century R&B crooners.

Even without the events swirling around the murders in Toni's family, "Crossroad" would have been a memorable song in my life. The murders amplified its resonance, but it's the quality of the song that has sustained its permanence in my mind.

The fact that it was my younger brother who prompted me to think about "Crossroad" has also greatly influenced my impressions of the song. Randy's allusion to "Crossroad" stuck with me because it was after that conversation that I noticed that not only was I helping him during this crisis but he was also helping me. I was helping him deal with the immediacy of death and the end of his relationship with Toni. And he helped me see that I wasn't fulfilling my own responsibilities as his older brother. I kept Randy's secret without being more diligent about finding out exactly what kind of environment he was traveling in. I exposed Randy to an unnecessary risk and I would have been deeply saddened if he had been hurt. As our conversations evolved from talking about the murders to talking about our own relationship, words like "shock," "hurt," and "fear" were now being replaced with "trust," "openness," and "honesty." More important, the deaths in Toni's family forced my brother and me to realize that we had a relationship to keep alive with roles and responsibilities for each of us.

8. "ROMIE" / Beenie Man

Beenie Man's "Romie" has been a favorite song of mine from the moment I heard it in the spring of 1997. I have always dug the song because of the pulse-tingling track highlighted by Beenie's signature callback—"Oh, nana, nana, na"—which propels the chorus. All of this sets in motion Beenie's chant about his nemesis Romie and his "whoring" sister Naomi, whom Beenie aspires to topple once and for all. The deep bass, sharp cymbal, and keyboard drops make the track as audacious as Beenie's attacks on his foes.

"Romie" has taken on a life of its own among my friends, some of whom will gladly tell anyone who will listen about the night in 1997 when I morphed from mild-mannered Ferentz, budding Ph.D., to Da Mayor, Dance Hall Don Supreme lickin' nuff shots in de classroom, BUP! BUP! BUP! Okay, I'll stop now. The incident in question took place when I went clubbing in the Village with three colleagues from a New York University summer program. When we hit the dance floor at one spot, the legendary Webster Hall, we were playing it cool. At least I know I was. I was the sole New Yorker in the group and I wanted to keep my wits about me to make sure my friends were having a good time. I had already done a good job of getting us from one place to another without incident and getting us into Nell's past bouncers who might have thought that our nerdy, broke-ass-student presence might not befit their club.

About twenty minutes after we arrived at Webster Hall, my friends and I were settled in on the hip-hop/reggae floor. The four of us were dancing in a circle, going through the paces of yet another rap set. Then the deejay began playing dancehall and everyone immediately became more animated. The women loosened their hips, and me and my friend Darren followed their lead. We interspersed a bit of wining into the two-steps that we were doing. The deejay was running through a Super Cat mix and I needed the space to get open to these early '90s dancehall jams. I backed away from my dance partner, Kira, and high stepped through "Ghetto Red Hot," a dancehall toast about the volatile nature of life in Kingston's trench towns. My high stepping was more pronounced when "Don Dada," Super Cat's boasting chant about his prowess, came on. Kira and I both enjoyed the popular playboy toast "Dem No Worry We," on which Heavy D also appears, and were already beginning to get closer to each other when the deejay switched from that lighthearted romp to Mad Cobra's 1992 erotic thrill piece "Flex," a slow, lilting, raw exploration of, well, sex. Taking our cue from Mad Cobra, Kira and I were now skin to skin on the dance floor, our pelvises slinking along with each other in slow, timid movements. I was apprehensive about dancing this intimately with Kira because we were still more like colleagues and had yet to really become friends.

My apprehensions gradually subsided the more that Kira relaxed into my body. The easing tension could be felt in our now looser hips that were fluidly revolving in unison. Kira then turned around and fixed her backside to my pelvis, which more than welcomed the opportunity to play host. Then all of a sudden the deejay threw on Beenie Man's "Romie." I don't know what I did but when he played "Romie," I felt Kira tense up and noticed my two other friends shooting glances in my direction. At first I tried playing it cool, backed away from Kira, and went into the low-key hand-clap two-step dance that I had been doing during the rap set. Then the next thing I knew I unbuttoned my shirt and took hold of Kira in what since then has always been referred to as "da dance."

Kira, who's about five foot one and a drop over one hundred pounds, was standing across from me—all six foot three and two hundred pounds of me. I pulled her toward me, with so much force, I accidentally catapulted her on top of me.

"Imagine going from standing still one second and then being projected onto someone's chest the next second," is how she often describes it when recounting the story to friends. I couldn't stop. I didn't want to stop. For the rest of the song I did a smorgasbord of dancehall dances, bogling, pepperseeding, "an' all 'a dat" with her on my chest, holding on for dear life.

As soon as "Romie" ended, I simply put Kira down and went back to my two-step as if nothing had happened. Our friends stared in awe at what had taken place. Kira tried to collect herself.

By the end of our stay in the NYU program, this escapade grew to epic proportions. According to the legend, I didn't just unbutton my shirt, I ripped it open and flung it in the air. The two other West Indian students in the program, neither of whom had been present that night at the club, could not resist adding their two cents to the narrative. It was their contention that I had, like a participant in a voodoo ritual, been mounted that evening. When Rachelle, the woman doing research on Caribbean religions, explained that mounting was a term used to describe when a person gets possessed by a god and while under that god's influence performs acts that they otherwise might not have done, everyone in the room came to the consensus that Beenie's chant on "Romie" had the ability to possess me. And now when Kira tells the story, in addition to my having tossed her onto my chest, she says that I tossed her up in the air a few times, and in one instance that I did a split and popped back up before I caught her.

What made this transformation that much more remarkable was that we had been dancing with each other in a fairly predictable fashion for about three hours at the other clubs prior to arriving at Webster Hall, but we had only stayed for the hip-hop sets at the other clubs. So all that anyone had seen me do was soul-brother rap two-step, which is actually a no-step because the guy barely moves and leaves the real dancing to the lady.

Even my little "Don Dada" interlude during the Super

Cat and Mad Cobra mixes were fairly tame compared to what occurred when "Romie" came on. "Romie," which appears on Beenie Man's 1996 album *Maestro*, is a shot back at another deejay, Romie, who dissed Beenie on a record. It isn't even the most popular or infectious recording on *Maestro*; that designation is reserved for "Girls Dem Sugar," a song that four years later was still being remixed and making cameos on the pop charts. *Maestro* also features another one of my favorite Beenie Man songs, "Long Longi Lala," his collaboration with fellow dancehall artist Lady Saw. The dancehall equivalent of Lil' Kim, only rawer, Lady Saw has been the preeminent "rude girl" in a genre known primarily for its "rude boys" and their offerings. More recently, she's gained notoriety for her collaborations with pop group No Doubt on their *Billboard* hit "Underneath It All," where she reprised one of the verses from her own hit single "Sycamore Tree." While I would rank many of Lady Saw's slackness romps alongside Beenie Man's other offerings, no other song in her catalog, or his for that matter, is capable of challenging my irrepressible addiction to "Romie."

9. "VOCAB" / *the Fugees*

When a konpa record came on during my Haitian friends' parties when we were teenagers, the festivities would take an awkward turn. Konpa is Haiti's most popular musical genre, so the adults who had been preoccupied with talking to one another, playing dominoes, or attending to the cooking flooded the dance floor, dragging their sons and daughters along with them. As we danced with our mothers, aunts, uncles, or fathers, the non-Haitian kids at the party bided their time by either standing on the sidelines or trying to copy the konpa dance moves with a mishmash of salsa and merengue motions.

Just as everyone seemed to be enjoying the stirrings of konpa artists Tabou Combo, Skah Shah, or Sweet Micky, a dancehall record, usually requested by one of the non-Haitian guests during the konpa set, would come on, and the non-Haitian kids were back on the floor. As this wave of boglers and pepperseeders sent our parents back to their chairs, there was always that one parent, furious at being rushed off the floor, defiantly declaring, "So you think you're Jamaican now!" This comment was leveled in the direction of her or his child, but applied to all of us Haitian kids who were either born in the States or emigrated at very early ages and who shared our American and West Indian friends' tastes in music. Each time this happened we were all reminded that while we thought we were just like other kids who had different tastes in music than their parents, our parents were far more concerned that their children might have different tastes in cultures.

I was able to limit the occurrence of these awkward moments by listening primarily to Haitian music in the company of my parents or other family members. When the music was turned down during these listening sessions, it was because Dad or one of my uncles wanted to tell stories about his days as a mack in the '60s and '70s. They relished each and every opportunity to talk about watching bands like Orchestra Tropicana and Les Fantaisistes de Carrefour evolve from a group of guys they went to school with or knew from their neighborhood in Petion Ville to becoming superstars in Haiti. I imagined these tales being akin to what my American friends' parents were telling them about their heydays in Detroit or Philadelphia as Motown and Philadelphia International were taking shape. And I thought my West Indian friends' parents had their own tales about liming around with Bob Marley or the Mighty Sparrow before these two men ascended to international acclaim.

I longed for the day when my Haitian friends and I would

have our own Bob Marley to attract our non-Haitian friends to konpa, rara, or any of the other forms of Haitian music. Until then, we investigated rumors that some of the more popular artists of the early '90s like Grand Puba, Al B. Sure!, and Tevin Campbell were Haitian. (Yes, *that* Tevin Campbell.) There was rarely any rhyme or reason to these rumors, but we still looked into them just in case they might be true. I thought I should've been able to put this habit to rest when Milli Vanilli arrived on the scene and there were rumors that they were Haitian too; not only were they not Haitian but they weren't even singers. When my friend Will picked up on my act, it became our running joke in all conversations about celebrities: "Michael Jordan, oh yeah, he's Haitian. His name is actually Michel Jourdain but he changed it for endorsement purposes."

Will and I became so predictable that our friends often beat us to the punch with our own joke, which is what I thought my friend Dennis was doing when he dropped by my parents' apartment one day with a tape for me to listen to. "Fo, this shit is hot," Dennis declared as he handed me his Walkman. "I'm telling you," smacking his right fist into his left palm as he waited for me to slip on the headphones, "these niggas is dope." No sooner did I press play than my face scrunched as if I had just bitten into a lemon. "D., what the fuck is this?"

Having grown up on the slick production of hip-hop wizards Marley Marl and DJ Premier, the acoustic guitar that Fugees members Wyclef Jean and Prakazrel Michel rhyme over on "Vocab," the single that Dennis had on his Walkman, was foreign to my ears. I associated acoustic guitars with Tracy Chapman and John Denver. It would have been one thing to rap over an acoustic guitar sample, but to arrange a whole song around one was rap heresy in my mind. Dennis, on the other hand, thought all of this was amusing. He had collapsed under the weight of his laughter and was bracing himself against the wall in our building's hallway.

"Those are your people!" Dennis declared, all the while pointing his index finger at me as if he were placing a hex on me. Dennis's antics reminded me of the harassment at school when films depicting Haitians as barbaric villains or exotic voodoo-spewing psychopaths gave my classmates an arsenal of material for derogatory Haitian jokes. This scene is actually exquisitely captured in the "Da Kid from Haiti Interlude" appearing on the Fugees' debut album *Blunted on Reality*, where Michel and Jean are dissed by a group of girls they try kicking it to. The interlude begins with Jean whispering something to one of the girls. Their conversation proceeds along smoothly until she discovers that he's Haitian, at which point she and the rest of the girls immediately announce their distaste. The interlude concludes with one of the girls declaring, "I'm sorry. I just can't be talkin' to no fuckin' Haitians."

At the time, I thought "Vocab" was one of the worst rap songs I'd ever heard, and consequently the Fugees were one of the worst trios ever. Worse yet I soon discovered that Michel and Jean are the only two Haitian members of the Fugees, and along with being the two Haitians, I also thought they were the two lesser emcees.

"Damn, y'all Haitians can't even rhyme better than a girl," was Dennis's persistent comment as the Fugees became a recurring topic of conversation after the release of "Nappy

Heads," a more lyrical, but still very uneven, song on *Blunted on Reality*.

Michel and Jean, whose cadence on the album version of "Vocab" practically runs counter to the melody, took the brunt of the abuse in these conversations. They sound as if they are *barreling* over guitar chords rather than *rhyming* over them. And then there're the verses, which upon initial listen don't make sense. They're performing a lyrical vocabulary exercise without any regard to plot or subject.

When Jean and Michel speed up their rhymes, the influence of other rap groups like Poor Righteous Teachers (PRT) and Lords of the Underground (LOU) becomes evident. Like PRT and LOU, the Fugees were also formed in New Jersey in the early '90s. LOU, the toasters who in 1993 gave us *Here Come the Lords* and infectious hits like "Chief Rocka" and "Here Come the Lords," deftly straddled the divide between funk-filled abstract wordsmithery and Dr. Dre–ish chronic gangsta funk. The then immeasurable popularity of LOU partially explains why Jean and Michel chose to emulate the rapport between Mr. Funke and Doitall, especially when the two Fugees lower their voices an octave or two and inject a few grains of grittiness.

PRT, fronted by Wise Intelligent and spurred on by the success of their 1990 album, *Holy Intellect*, which featured the hit "Rock Dis Funky Joint," was the first of these three groups to make an impact in the music industry. Like KRS-One had previously displayed during his tenure with Boogie Down Productions, PRT once again proved that with the right front man a group could capitalize on blending jazz, reggae, and rap—even if the rhymes have political overtones. When Jean is chanting toward the end of "Vocab" one hears glimpses of Wise Intelligent, who himself rarely ever rapped on a record, preferring instead to deliver his rhymes in a sped-up dancehall-like cadence. Unlike his fore-bears, KRS-One and Wise Intelligent, Jean's riddim toward the end of "Vocab" lacks the fluidity that makes their stylings enjoyable.

Even Lauryn Hill, the third member of the Fugees and the woman who would later challenge Mary J. Blige for the hip-hop and R&B throne, also sounds as if she's audition-ing for either PRT or LOU on "Vocab," although she is more in tune with the guitar than her male counterparts. Her solo is anchored by the refrain "What's the matter with the black man?" Hill offers a complexly articulated com-mentary on violence among black men, disrespect for black women, and the misguided excuses people make to explain away these behaviors. While not necessarily stellar, Hill's wee bit of lyrical context helps redeem the song.

I did my best to defend the Fugees. Still, other than a few bright spots on "Nappy Heads," *Blunted on Reality* didn't give me much to work with. I feared that if the Fugees didn't succeed as a group they'd quickly be discarded by the music industry and the public's lasting impression of them would be the two Haitian front men with subpar flows. The mod-erate success of *Blunted on Reality* gave the Fugees a second chance to make a record and to showcase their maturity as artists. They undoubtedly made the most of this second chance by producing their innovative landmark 1996 album, *The Score*—which for a period was the best-selling rap album of all time.

Two years later in 1996 while listening to Funkmaster Flex's radio show on New York's Hot 97 during my sophomore year at Queens College (CUNY), I heard the beginning of what I thought was Roberta Flack's pristine "Killing Me Softly." My first thought was that Flack must have passed away, or something else tragic had happened to her, because I couldn't figure out why Flex would be playing this soulful classic on his hip-hop program. Then I heard it, that trumpet flare from the Roy Ayers sample used six years earlier on A Tribe Called Quest's single "Bonita Applebum." Except this time the sample did not usher in Q-Tip's abstract poetics; it preceded a simple effervescent greeting from Jean. Jean peppers this updated version of "Killing Me Softly" with sprinkles of youthful energy that distinguish it from its predecessor and anything else that was on the radio at the time. (The lone possible exception was "I'll Be There for You/You're All I Need to Get By," Mary J. Blige and Method Man's 1995 remake of Marvin Gaye and Tammi Terrell's 1968 hit ballad.)

"Killing Me Softly" has none of the dissonant vocals that appeared frequently on *Blunted on Reality*. Hill's performance on "Killing Me Softly" unveiled the stunning voice submerged beneath the gruff vocals on "Vocab." Her tender vocals rival Roberta Flack's original rendition, while also giving some credence to the lofty comparisons to Aretha Franklin that were being bandied about. I was surprised at myself for seeing the merits of this comparison, considering that only two years earlier she played a key role in the bizarro "Vocab."

The beat on "Killing Me Softly" was as important as Hill's vocals in making it a success. It took me back to 1990, back to the "old school," back to Jamaica High School and sitting in front of the "Black Irishman" Hassan O'Rourke as he banged out this beat on his desk. When Tribe copped this beat, which Ayers had produced for the group Ramp's song "Daylight," I thought hip-hop was on the verge of a new era in sound. Q-Tip's lust ballad seemed tailor-made for the effortless "ta-boom bip" bass and snare kicks seasoned with dashes of trumpet flares. By using the same beat as Tribe, the Fugees are also updating that anthem as well, injecting morsels of feminine maturity into that group's youthful masculine anthem. If "Bonita Applebum" is remembered as jazz and rap's first kiss after a prolonged courtship, then "Killing Me Softly" has to be regarded as the first time they made love.

I may have fallen in love with "Killing Me Softly" but it was "No Woman, No Cry," another song covered on *The Score*, that got me in trouble. During a discussion of the song, my classmate Eric obstinately railed at Jean for his audacity in attempting a cover of the legendary Bob Marley song. Jean's effort was borderline blasphemy, Eric asserted. When it came my turn to chime in, I started speaking meekly, unsure what my point really was. Yet as I spoke and noticed that those huddled around were listening intently, I grew more self-assured. While we may call Marley a "reggae" artist, I declared, his music cut across quite a few genres, including rock, country, ska, and rhythm and blues. This point people agreed with. In my self-assuredness, I got too ambitious and added, "Wyclef is a lot closer to Bob Marley than we give him credit for."

The way the others in our circle began registering their disbelief—"WHAT!??!!"—you would have thought I'd just told this group of black students that the KKK is simply misunderstood. Eric, the lanky Trinidadian student who had been denouncing Jean just a moment ago, took particular offense. He swung his arm so violently in objection to my contentions that he resembled a laborer striking at a cane stalk.

In hindsight, I can't really hold Eric's reaction against him. It's unfair to both Jean and Marley to make such a comparison. Jean had only two albums under his belt, and it was premature to try arguing that he was on the verge of accomplishing anything comparable to what Marley produced during his musical career. Nonetheless, I couldn't help but be moved enough by his cover of "No Woman, No Cry."

Jean's rendition is an elegy for loved ones who passed away too soon. He deftly outlines the setting: the government yards of New Jersey and Brooklyn, the two areas where he grew up. From there he alludes to the senseless violence that has robbed him of friends and the mourning rituals practiced by young people that reflect their inexperience with death.

While he doesn't have Marley's singing prowess, Jean does share his proficiency with the guitar. Jean's gentle chords tug at one's heart with the same little-boy earnestness that makes his forever crackling voice so enjoyable. This ballad, dedicated to "all the Refugees worldwide," was another step in Jean's evolution from fledging Haitian rapper to internationally acclaimed artist and activist, a passage that culminated with the 1997 release of his solo album, *The Carnival*. As the Fugees', then Jean's, popularity increased, the derogatory comments about Haitians decreased. These epithets were now being replaced with a level of praise and sensible interest in Haitian culture that I'd never experienced before. Haitians quickly became the new Jamaicans and were receiving praise across the board. The same guys who used to scream "booloo, booloo, booloo," to mimic Kreyol were now greeting me on the block with "*Sak passé*," the Kreyol term for "What's up."

My dad wasn't as generous when it came to Jean. When I played the three Kreyol tracks from *Carnival*—"Jaspora," "Yele," and "Carnival"—for him, he dismissed Jean's attempts at mixing konpa and hip-hop. He bristled at what he saw as the "hoodlumish" nature of Jean's sound. In Dad's view, Jean was a "Haitian artist," but his songs were not "Haitian music."

Taken aback by his comments, I pushed him to elaborate on what he meant, especially given that my dad was only a few years away from joining Jean as a Haitian who had spent a greater portion of his life living abroad than he had in Haiti. In truth, I wasn't pressing Dad just to get his thoughts on Jean; I wanted his opinion on young Haitians in general.

With Jean's music playing as Dad and I sat next to each other, I heard how young Jean was, how young I was, and realized that he was just beginning to scratch the surface in his mission to blend the sounds of the Caribbean with those of the United States. I realized that he and I were engaged in a similar struggle to convince our Haitian elders that by embracing aspects of African American and Caribbean cultures we were not turning our backs on Haiti. We were instead doing what Haitian artists from novelist Jacques Roumain to contemporary chanteuse Emeline Michel had always done—simply seeking to assert our rightful place in the African diaspora. If I hadn't been so intent on making sure that our discussion did not turn into an argument, I would have challenged Dad's notion of "Haitian music" by asking him to explain how Jean's decision to blend rap with konpa, salsa, and zouk was different from konpa musicians incorporating meringue, salsa, and zouk on their recordings.

This brought me back to "Vocab." At seventeen, it had been easy for me to write off "Vocab" as wack. I had very little insight into the hard work demanded of an artist trying to get their vision across. When I revisited "Vocab" at twenty-one with ears and a worldview that had matured considerably, I picked up more of Jean's and Michel's puns, and discovered that their muffled voices sometimes parodied the deep baritone often held up as the model of masculinity. I heard the yearnings of two men who weren't necessarily trying to emulate other rappers, but who were urgently trying to hold on to an opportunity that they had long coveted, two men trying to make the most of a dream. Listening to the song again, I happened upon this verse by Jean that I had long overlooked:

> . . . *said my music wouldn't make F.M.*
> *Station. You're Haitian.*

Jean's defiant response to the radio programmer was the dream that many of my Haitian friends shared, where one day we'd be hearing one of our own on FM radio. We wanted our people to have a place front and center and not be relegated to Sunday-morning shows on AM radio or random late-night spots. After years of bemoaning the existence of "Vocab," I eventually got it. Their vocab had been my own.

10. "HAPPY BIRTHDAY" / *Stevie Wonder*

Eight years ago I was blessed with the chance to travel to Durban, South Africa. I went as part of the first class of students in the International Winter School at the University of Natal, Durban (UND). At first I was nervous about how my experience in Durban would turn out. When I went to register for classes, I learned that there was only one other student in the program and she was a local UND student, an Indian woman. With this in mind, I did my best not to stand out as an American.

As I walked around in my black Phat Farm rugby shirt, blue jeans, and Nike hiking boots, I could feel the eyes staring at me. I felt like kicking myself each time someone said, "How's it" (the local way of saying hello). Instead of returning the same greeting, I cast a head nod in their direction.

Needless to say, my efforts to not stand out as an American weren't going particularly well.

Yet, in no time I found myself uttering Durban's two most common greetings—"How's it" and "Yebo"—to everyone who walked by and took every opportunity to pepper the UND students with questions about growing up in South Africa during apartheid. They in turn asked me how it felt growing up under Ronald Reagan. I asked them what they thought about Mandela, and they mined me for my thoughts on Dr. Martin Luther King Jr. and Malcolm X—and why was Mandela still walking this earth while his two peers had been assassinated? Our conversations were now gaining enough depth that guys whom I had known for less than three weeks were feeling like lifelong friends. This feeling resonated deeply when our conversations turned to music.

We'd spend hours on the benches in front of the university batting around thoughts about Michael Jackson, Tupac Shakur, and the Notorious B.I.G. as the Indian Ocean rustled off in the distance. Mention of these three artists usually sent someone off into a lament about how death—or in Jackson's case eccentricity—devours the young and gifted. Artists like Bob Marley and Marvin Gaye were so revered that they seemed more alive than many of the contemporary artists we heard on the radio. The UND students talked about them almost daily and wore T-shirts emblazoned with Marley's face. Of course, once Marley and Gaye were mentioned and the focus of the conversation became politically active musicians, it was only a matter of seconds before Stevie Wonder's name was brought up.

The graduate students were particularly fond of Wonder. Mostly in their mid- to late twenties, they were the last generation to really come of age under apartheid, which had ended just eight years earlier, in 1990. When they talked about Wonder, their eyes lit up as they remembered hearing broadcasts of his songs and reading his comments denouncing apartheid, all of which made them feel as if they weren't being abandoned in their crusade. And their excitement had reached a high point this season because Stevie was going to be in town in a few weeks to headline a benefit concert.

One of the UND graduate students, Thando, was especially thrilled about the upcoming performance. He had followed Wonder's career for years and couldn't contain his excitement over seeing him in concert for the first time. He also couldn't understand why I wasn't as excited or committed to attending the performance since I'd also never seen Wonder perform. To me a concert was a concert, no matter who was performing. I wasn't even committed to attending.

Every time Thando saw me on campus, he'd throw his right fist in the air, a habit that he once told me meant hello and that he was ready for the revolution. Thando wasn't taking classes that semester, but was working a variety of jobs on campus that required him to be there every day. Before I knew it, he became my consistent lunch companion. We developed a routine where I picked up some samosas from the Indian food cart on campus and he brought two servings of whatever lunch they provided in his office, along with a CD for me to listen to. Through Thando I became acquainted with Miriam Makeba, Lucky Dube, and Hugh Masekela, a few of South Africa's most revered musical artists.

One Monday in July I brought the samosas but Thando didn't show up for lunch. It was weird, because even though

I had known this man for less than three weeks, I had already accepted him as a fixture in my life. I ate my samosas and walked around campus thinking that I might bump into him before class, to no avail. At about 6:00 PM when I was about to leave campus for the day, I heard someone calling me from the steps of the History Department building: "Ferentz! Ferentz!"

It was Thando. He gave me his trademark raised-fist sign, patted the person that he was speaking to on her arm, and then broke into a sprint toward me. He was a sight running in his multicolored vest, his locks bouncing off his light blue denim shirt. When he reached me he said, "How's it?" and started trying to catch his breath. Reaching into his pocket he pulled out two tabs—"BAM!"—and stuck them in front of my face. At first I couldn't make out what was written on the ticket, especially since Thando was too hyper to keep his arm still for me to read them. I bobbed my head up and down trying to keep pace with his arm. It was of no use. "What are they?" I asked.

"Bro! These are two tickets to see Stevie. One for you and one for me. So now you have to go."

I didn't know what to say. "Thank you," I meekly declared as he let me hold the tickets to look them over. "How much do I owe you?" I asked him while reading the ticket stubs.

"Nothing. It's my way of saying thanks for all the samosas."

I conceded and accepted the ticket. As we ate lunch that week, all Thando could talk about was the concert. Each day I absorbed more of his excitement. Each day the caravan of people whom we were going to taxi to the concert with grew larger and larger. It seemed that every time someone walked by, Thando asked them, "Are you going to see Stevie?" The answer was inevitably, "Yes," just as Thando's reply was, "Good, then we'll go together." I had so deeply adopted Thando's zeal for going to see Stevie that it was not until we got to the show, which was held at an outdoor stadium in Durban, that I realized that there were other acts on the bill, Dru Hill and LL Cool J.

When Wonder took the stage all the older people who had been sitting on blankets toward the back of the gallery during Dru Hill's and Cool J's perfomances rose to their feet and walked toward the front. As he went through his set, we all did our best to sing each song word for word, and when we couldn't we made up words so that we would at least look like we were singing along with him.

The song that stands out for me during this performance was Wonder's rendition of "Happy Birthday." It had not really sunk in until he began singing it that the concert was part of Nelson Mandela's eightieth birthday celebration. Even though Mandela was not in attendance, the sight of Stevie Wonder accompanied by five thousand or so people serenading Mandela on his birthday was an unforgettable experience. As an African American participating in this choir, the tragic irony of Martin Luther King's death came to life. Watching Wonder sing the song he had written to build support for a King national holiday during the birthday ceremony for Mandela, or as he is affectionately known in South Africa, Madiba—an honorary title bestowed upon esteemed Xhosa elders—was eye-opening.

"Happy Birthday" originally appeared on Wonder's 1980 album, *Hotter Than July*, the second album he released after *Songs in the Key of Life*, the other being the 1979 soundtrack to a never-released movie, *Journey Through the Secret Life of Plants*. Along with "Happy Birthday," *Hotter Than July* also featured the songs "Master Blaster 'Jammin,' " a hard-hitting reggae experiment; "All I Do," an up-tempo disco/soul-meets-rock track; and "Lately," a heart-wrenching ballad.

I guess it must've been when I only started hearing Wonder's "Happy Birthday" sung at birthday parties that I began losing sight of the fact that it was written for King. I wasn't even in the United States yet when *Hotter Than July* came out and don't remember Wonder singing "Happy Birthday" at an event associated with King until the 1986 celebration marking the first observance of Martin Luther King Day. By this time, the struggle to have a holiday recognizing King's contributions was almost twenty years old. The crusade began shortly after King's death in 1968, when Michigan representative John Conyers introduced a bill in Congress promoting the holiday, a bill that was not passed until 1983, and it wasn't until 2000 that it was observed by its official name as a paid holiday in all fifty states.

When Wonder released "Happy Birthday," he was bringing attention to the work initiated by Conyers and union organizers who used the cause to galvanize their members. King had a strong following among union members because of the work that he did on their behalf; he was assassinated while in Memphis in support of striking sanitation workers. After "Happy Birthday" was released, the song was adopted as the anthem for the King holiday movement and began Wonder's ascent to the fore of this movement for which he hosted the 1981 Rally for Peace Press Conference in Washington, D.C.

Written and produced by Wonder, "Happy Birthday" is both celebratory and insightful. The light shaking of the maracas in the background coupled with the regaling chant of "Happy birthday to ya" evokes cheer and good times. Meanwhile, the thoughtful lyrics about King, his worthiness for a national holiday, and the rolling synthesizer and drum loops bring out more serious elements. In a sense, "Happy Birthday" is part chant and part anthem, a sing-along testimonial to the importance of King's life and convictions.

It also has taken on a life as the "black folk's version" of "Happy Birthday," a more "soulful" way of singing the traditional serenade. During this serenade, the chorus is simply repeated and the testimony to King is left out. There is sometimes a kind word or two about the person being feted, but that's not essential. This was the version of "Happy Birthday" that I had become used to and which I was prepared to hear Wonder sing that night in Durban. Instead, he went through the original, singing King's praises and leaving us to trail behind as best as we could. Then he changed it up on the second verse. Instead of continuing to sing about King, he adapted the song for Madiba; this change drove the crowd wild. When the chorus came around this time, the entire stadium was singing along "Happy birthday to ya. Happy birthday to ya. Happy birthday, Madiba."

It felt exhilarating being swept up by the crowd's energy. While chanting the chorus I caught a glimpse of Thando happily pumping his right fist in the air as he sang along with everyone else. When he noticed me looking at him he gave me a gentle nudge on the shoulder with his elbow and put his left arm around me. We both stood there rocking back and forth gleefully singing "Happy birthday, Madiba."

While writing about the concert in my journal the next morning my mind drifted back to the conversations that I had had with graduate students a few weeks earlier. As I started coming off from the previous night's high, my euphoria morphed into thoughts of how bittersweet Wonder's rousing tribute to Mandela was. Standing in that stadium thirty years after King's murder and taking part in a ceremony to honor one of his contemporaries served as another reminder of how Mandela's imprisonment and King's assassination sent my peers in South Africa and me in the United States on divergent paths. They came of age fighting for their liberation from under the reins of apartheid; meanwhile, I was being instructed that the civil rights movement ended in the '60s. While they were marching for Mandela's release from prison in the '80s, I was writing letters in support of an official day to honor King. For my entire life these two icons have always been distinguishable by one overwhelming fact: one was still alive, while the other had been dead for almost a decade by the time I was born.

Meditating on Wonder's performance that morning, particularly when he exchanged Mandela's name for King's during "Happy Birthday," the song's tragic irony was again evident; while it honors King's birth and his life, it is a reminder of his death. Wonder's insertion of Mandela's name into the melody magnified the weight of this realization, which was fortunately tempered by the crowd's reaction to his switch. The excitement permeating the stadium as we sang "Happy Birthday" to Mandela was undoubtedly generated by the fact that he was still alive to enjoy his birthday, just like those of us in attendance were still alive and capable of continuing the struggle he has endured while honoring the memory of his deceased counterpart.

11. "PORTUGUESE LOVE" / *Teena Marie*

The first time I heard Teena Marie's "Portuguese Love," I was about to pick up Tricia from Union Station in New Haven. I discovered the song online earlier that day and had been playing it nonstop most of the afternoon. While this was not as bad as when your favorite song comes on the radio just as you pull into your driveway, forcing you to make the decision whether you have enough time to get the groceries out of the trunk, run inside, and turn on the radio before the song goes off the air, I was hooked enough to consider asking Tricia to take a cab home.

I would've done it too except that it was her car and she'd been away for a week. Therefore, if I wanted some Afro-American lovin' when she got home, I needed to get to that train station pronto. When I got the call from her that they had just pulled into a nearby stop, I grabbed the copy of

"Portuguese Love" that I had just burned onto a CD and jetted down to the station.

The train station was about a five-minute drive from our house, and usually the trip went by without incident. The light at the corner of Tower Parkway and Broadway drove me mad because it stands at the heart of a roundabout, and if you miss it, you have to wait for traffic in the other two directions to take their turn before the light changes again in your favor. Since I had Teena Marie in the car with me that day, though, that light could have taken an hour, no, a week to change and it wouldn't have bothered me a bit. Unfortunately, I missed the light and with it went my plan to pick up some flowers for Tricia. A big hug and smile from her boo would have to do.

Sitting at the light I noticed that on one side of me was a car with three black women, and on the other, a station wagon with a white couple. I wanted to make sure that they weren't paying attention to my singing along to "Portuguese Love" as if I were in my own house. Both parties were facing forward, eagerly waiting for the light to change. Normally I would've been just as preoccupied with the light as they were, but with the best four minutes of music in history under way, that light was the last thing on my mind.

"Portuguese Love" first appeared on Marie's 1981 album, *It Must Be Magic*, which was her last album for Motown, ending a three-year relationship that firmly established Marie's roots in black music. The song tells the story of a vibrant love affair between a woman and her Portuguese lover, bolstered by a lively keyboard track and eclectic percussion arrangement that switches back and forth from a snare set to djembe drums. When the pace speeds up toward the end of the song, Marie's voice concedes the spotlight to her background musicians, who treat listeners to a rousing alto saxophone improv. The tone of the instrumentation shifts as Marie's tale goes from her passionate yearning for her lover to coming undone by the overwhelming memories of their exhilarating nights together. Marie also infuses "Portuguese Love" with specks of scatting reminiscent of Latin jazz vocalists Tito Puente, Celia Cruz, and Marie's namesake, Brazilian artist Tânia Maria.

Most know Marie because of her association with Rick James, her mentor and lover during her early years at Motown. The two sang the unforgettable duet "Fire and Desire," recorded for James's 1981 LP *Street Songs*. He wrote most of the selections on Marie's 1979 debut album, *Wild and Peaceful*, but by the time her second album, *Lady T*, came out in 1980 James's partnership with Marie had ended. Having achieved a modicum of success at Motown, Marie was now asserting herself as an artist and taking more control of her career. This meant writing most of the songs on her subsequent albums and eventually producing and arranging her final two Motown albums, *Irons in the Fire* and *It Must Be Magic*. The success of *It Must Be Magic* was driven by "Square Biz," the song later sampled by rap group the Firm (AZ, Foxy Brown, Nas, and Nature) on their recording "Firm Biz." While her recordings continue to have a central place in the Motown catalog, *It Must Be Magic* was the best-selling of Marie's Motown quartet.

Judging from my initial response to "Portuguese Love," it makes sense that it appeared on an album entitled *It Must Be Magic*. Sitting in the car, I fell under Marie's spell over and over again. As Marie got closer and closer to the song's climax, so did I. I tapped more deliberately on the steering wheel, cocking my head back, pulling myself into the steering column as she hit each note. As the song drew to a close and the last echoes of her voice fluttered alongside the sounds of the sax, I turned to my fellow drivers. My entire performance had been observed. Judging by the smiles in the cars on both sides of me, it was appreciated by all. I gave the voyeurs a smile and slowly pulled out of my lane when the light changed.

When I met Tricia at the train station, I was so spent after my encounter with Teena Marie that I asked her to drive us home. I wanted to fully immerse myself in the afterglow and rest so that I could be ready in case I got another chance to reexperience "Portuguese Love" later that evening.

12. "AS" / *Stevie Wonder*
AND "YOU ARE MY HEAVEN" /
Roberta Flack and Donny Hathaway

The weekend after I proposed to Tricia, we headed to New York and Toronto to celebrate with our respective families. This spurt of traveling proved useful because it gave us our first chance as an engaged couple to brainstorm about the details of our wedding. Soon the conversation about location, size, and budget became too overwhelming, so we started talking about our "music registry," the music we were going to play at the reception.

Our plan for our registry was simple. We wanted to make sure to incorporate elements from our respective cultures, so we were going to have sounds from Haiti, Eritrea, and the United States put in the mix. We relished the idea of adding music from places we had either traveled to or wanted to travel to: Brazil, Cape Verde, Nigeria, Ghana, England, and Jamaica were invited to this musical world cup.

In short, we wanted our reception to be an African diaspora soul shakedown.

Logically we needed to find a deejay capable of handling the task. That's right, long before we had a location, a caterer, or anything else, we were going to have a deejay. Choosing the deejay early was extremely important because we knew that the earlier we asked, the more likely we were to get the deejay we wanted. This also gave us ample time to work with him or her to ensure that all the songs we wanted would make it onto our playlist.

One guy in particular, a friend of Tricia's from college, used to deejay in Atlanta back when house music ruled the ATL and on every second Saturday, Earwax was the place to be. It was through hearing Tricia's stories about her college crew's deep appreciation for soul house music that I was reacquainted with the genre. Back then I primarily associated house music with the clubs in New York, like Bentley's and Shelter, that my friends and I were too young to get into when house was thriving in the early '90s. In fact, to this day I still refer to most of the house music tracks I like as "that ol' Bentley's joint," even though I never set foot inside the establishment.

Of all of these "ol' Bentley's joints," the one that stands out the most is "Follow Me," by Aly-Us. It has an infectious refrain that echoes a plea to a loved one, be it a plea to follow you in love, revolution, or simply down the block; it is hard to imagine this message being expressed any better than it is on this song. Therefore when Tricia mentioned that she was going to ask her friend Tarik to deejay the reception, I immediately threw "Follow Me" onto our music registry for the night. We had no plans of turning our wedding reception into a house party, so "Follow Me" would have to suffice as the fix for the house-heads in attendance, especially since we knew the '60s and '70s were going to take up much of the registry and that we needed to be as thorough as possible in making our selections from these time periods. Half of her family hailed from "The D!"— Detroit. And as everyone knows there are two things that people in Detroit do not play with: their cars and their music.

It was a bit humbling the first time I met her family and tried to blend in by dropping names like James Brown, Aretha Franklin, and Rick James as musicians I had listened to when I was growing up. Tricia's mom and her aunt Rachel took off laughing. When her aunt collected herself, she offered to teach me more about "SOUL muuzzik" before I made this same mistake in front of Tricia's uncle and ruined my standing in the family before I'd even become a part of it. Through my conversation with these women I learned about artists such as Carmen McRae, Eartha Kitt, and Jackie Wilson, all of whom used to make them swoon back in the day. After hearing them talk about old-school Detroit and black music, I was pleasantly surprised that the three of us shared a guilty pleasure, Teena Marie's "Portuguese Love."

The other genre that had to be well represented was konpa. During my weekly conversations with my parents, I consulted with them over a list of songs for our music registry. Through collaborating with my parents and scouring konpa message boards, I rediscovered old classics and came across new gems that were sure to set the party afire. One such find was a song called "Min Medikaman-an," by the group T-Viçe.

In English, the song title means "Here's the Medicine." I remember putting the song on one day and dancing with Tricia in our living room, just like my mom and dad used to dance with each other in our old apartment. As "Min Medikaman-an" played in the background, I twirled Tricia around. After our dance, I explained the words to Tricia, konpa is the medicine for all of one's ills. As Tricia often did at the time, she exclaimed, "That one is definitely going on the registry," and ran to the nearest notepad to make sure it was marked down.

Along with konpa, I was responsible for making sure that the deejay knew to play reggae/dancehall classics like Foxy Brown's "Sorry," Shabba Ranks and Krystal's "Twice My Age," Super Cat's "Don Dada," and Beenie Man's "Romie."

Other than a few more recent selections by Mos Def, Talib Kweli, and De La Soul, whose *Stakes Is High* album Tricia and I listened to religiously when we first started dating in 1998, "Scenario" and "Da Choice Is Yours" were the only two rap songs guaranteed to make our registry. Space was limited and we wanted to pack in songs that would keep people dancing. We had three cultures and four continents to cover, which meant that much of the music from rap's golden age of the late '80s to early '90s, music we had grown up listening to, might not make the cut.

Tricia felt that I should make a similar concession to "Romie"; since it deals with violence and has nothing to do with love, she felt it wasn't appropriate for a wedding celebration. I proclaimed that either I added "Romie" to the playlist or R. Kelly's "Feelin' on Yo Booty," at which point Tricia made another dash to the clipboard on the refrigerator door and put "Romie" on the list.

We learned a lot about each other through these conversations about music. It was almost as if we had just started dating all over again, each conversation about a favorite song yielding another story and a new treasure about the other person: even those stories that had been previously recounted, like the one about the first party we attended together in graduate school where I spurned her invite to dance to the Commodores classic "Brickhouse."

Eventually, Tricia and I had compiled a list of almost two hundred songs. The list was so long that it looked as if we would need to have one of the old-world East African or Haitian wedding ceremonies lasting a week to have enough time to play all the music we wanted to hear. In spite of selecting such a long list of songs, we had yet to decide on "our" song, the one we would use for our first dance.

We seriously considered Stevie Wonder's "As." We'd developed a deep fondness for the song as a result of listening to it at her parents' house or on the car stereo during countless road trips. At the risk of sounding like two *American Bandstand* judges, Tricia and I thought "As" had a good beat and was easy to dance to (so we gave it a ten). Wonder's pronouncements on the nature of true love made it even more ideal for a wedding celebration: "As today I know I'm living but tomorrow / Could make me the past but that I mustn't fear." While Wonder is talking about life and death here, he is also talking about being present with love.

Knowing that some of our family members traveling in from abroad wouldn't understand the nuances of Wonder's mystical proclamations, Tricia and I appreciated that "As" was set to a series of cymbal clangs and coy piano runs that make it easy to dance to. We knew that whether they spoke English, Kreyol, or Tgrinya, our families could still relate to Wonder's energy, which according to his philosophy on music, transcends language, place, and time. And more personally, she and I thought the praise heaped on everlasting love was exactly the spirit we wanted to engender during the ceremony.

Even with all of these stellar qualities, we sadly decided against choosing "As" since it was used in *The Best Man*, a movie that many of our friends had seen. Tricia and I wanted something that would feel more original.

Maybe it was because we were placing a lot of attention on it, but Tricia and I felt unnerved by the fact that we had yet to find a song. Looking back on it, our preoccupation with the song kept our minds off the costs associated with the wedding and the difficulties that we were having securing a location.

Then, one afternoon, I was listening to an old-school collection passed along by a friend and a lovely tune came on. As I waited for the CD to download, Tricia walked in from work and rather than segue directly into the usual "How was your day" chatter, I took her in my arms and started dancing with her as we talked.

At one point Tricia asked, "Is this Donny?"

Sending her into a turn across the room that she accented with a ballroom dancer's flair, I replied, "Yes."

As she made her way back to me, she started to drift into one of her stories about a family outing in Detroit at which her uncle had played some of Donny Hathaway's music. Then, halfway into her story she suddenly stopped and cried out, "This is it! Ferentz, this is the song. This is it, baby!" She then gave me a kiss and took off running down the hall into the kitchen to write the song on the board.

When she came back into the study, she was still repeating, "This is it! We found it!" I thought she was referring to the song her uncle had played at the gathering back in the day.

"Aren't you excited?" she asked upon noticing that I wasn't as amped as she was. "Baby, we found our wedding song!"

In that instant it all connected and I replayed the song to see if I could hear it from her vantage point. It started out at a medium pace, giving us a chance to dance with a little pep from the jump, just like we wanted. And while the song doesn't speed up dramatically, it's still lively enough that English and non-English speakers alike could clap to it. After all, all that you have to do is follow the lead of the simulated clapping on the record. The fact that the song is not particularly long also made it attractive to us, because rather than have one song playing for a long time, "You Are My Heaven," by Donny Hathaway and Roberta Flack, would initiate a medley of songs that symbolized the assortment of spirits and cultures being brought together on our very special day.

Knowing how hard it was for us to decide on one song, we planned to have each set of parents pick a song that they would like to have played in the medley. We also decided to ask the maid of honor and the best man for contributions. That way all of the important parties at the wedding would get a chance to choose a song.

"You Are My Heaven" also stood out because it was a duet, and what better way to usher in our life together than to be serenaded by two of the most dynamic singers of the last thirty years. When paired on wax, Flack and Hathaway represented what Tricia and I aspired to be in our life together—magical, harmonious, tender, blissful, enduring, luminous, heavenly.

After we gave "You Are My Heaven" another spin, I was completely sold and was as excited as Tricia. We had finally found our song, or rather our song had found us. We played it over and over again for the rest of the evening, dancing to it before and after dinner, taking a break from watching TV to do a few twirls, and then dancing some more as Tricia called her parents to let them know that we'd settled on a song.

With our song in hand, Tricia and I could now plan the rest of the wedding.

13. "THIS WILL BE (AN EVERLASTING LOVE)" / *Natalie Cole*

Deidre, Elijah, and I met at Yale while they were in the law school and I was working on my Ph.D. It was also at Yale where they started dating. Our friendship really blossomed in 2003 when I moved into their neighborhood in Brooklyn. Elijah and I became teammates on a local basketball team, and once it became clear that I shared an interest in his beloved University of Texas Longhorns, we'd get together from time to time to watch college football. Meanwhile, Deidre appreciated my blissful ignorance when she tried setting me up with her friends. Surprisingly none of these single friends were positioned next to me at my table during their fall 2004 wedding—or so I think.

After alerting us that they were ready to make their entrance, the deejay announced the newlyweds and Deidre and Elijah walked arm in arm to the center of the dance floor where the spotlight was awaiting them. Elijah had on a classic black tux that hung neatly on his thin frame. Under the spotlight, the embroidery on Deidre's ivory dress sparkled brilliantly, accenting each of the gown's nuances: the subtle train at the end and the crisp angles in the neckline. They stood there waiting for the deejay to cue their music. The guests tapped on glasses, and Elijah gave Deidre a kiss. She sank into his arms until their song came on over the sound system.

By the way they were moving, I fully expected a slower number such as Stevie Wonder's "With a Song in My Heart" or Roberta Flack's "The First Time Ever I Saw Your Face" to come on. Instead, I was greeted by the piano run that ushers in Natalie Cole's "This Will Be (An Everlasting Love)," a spirited ballad that premiered in 1975 on her debut album *Inseparable*. It features a then twenty-five-year-old Cole vibrantly crooning and hollering about the joyous love that has entered her life.

Featuring an equally buoyant horn section, "This Will Be" was Cole's first major hit. The title sets up a call-and-response routine in which Cole plays the role of both the person issuing the call—"This will be"—and the imagined audience responding to her declaration—"an everlasting love." Deidre and Elijah's movements were perfectly in sync with the song's energy. Each turn, each dip was delivered perfectly on cue and accented by their smiles. They eschewed a standard two-step, displaying in its place a series of free-flowing moves that one might normally associate with swing dancing. They did their best impersonations of dance steps like the Charleston, the jitterbug, and a little cha-cha before inviting their wedding party and family members to join them on the dance floor.

Since we all were already on our feet in front of our chairs gleefully clapping along, I wasn't surprised when people who were not in the wedding party besieged the dance floor as well. I'll never forget this one duo in particular: a middle-aged white couple who I later discovered was one of Deidre's law school professors and his wife. They walked up right beside Deidre and Elijah and went straight into a ballroom dance routine in which they masterfully executed the same moves that the newlyweds had just attempted. Their performance drew uproarious applause.

When the deejay looped "This Will Be" for what had to be a third time, this older married couple and the newlyweds swapped partners. Elijah did his best to keep up with the law professor's wife, but I could tell that his eyes, like everyone else's in the hall, were on Deidre and her former professor, who was now twirling her around as he involved her in an elaborate salsa routine. As "This Will Be" finally drew to a close, our clapping morphed into further applause honoring the commitment that Deidre and Elijah had made before us, and the older couple who gave us a magnificently executed performance and some insight into how graceful an everlasting love might be.

14. "ROCK THE BELLS" / *LL Cool J* AND "99 PROBLEMS" / *Jay-Z*

One of my favorite movies of all time is *High Fidelity*, based on the Nick Hornby novel. I enjoyed that film because the musical debates and top-five lists fueling the banter between Barry (Jack Black) and Rob (John Cusack) remind me of the conversations with my male friends. Rob and Barry's frenetic dialogues in the film resemble the chaotic debates over the greatest album, band, and especially rapper of all time that my friends and I have been trying to settle for decades. When we're debating rappers, we're as dramatic and as comedic as Rob and Barry during their never-ending quest to list the five greatest albums for every situation in life.

I remember one time in particular during a trip to Rio for my friend Will's bachelor party in March 2004. Will's pending nuptials brought together a motley group of twelve made up of his friends from Queens and his alma mater, Howard University. As we sat around in the living room of the apartment waiting out an afternoon rainstorm, the conversation shifted from Will's wedding and our respective love lives to music, when we once again heard Will mumbling "now everybody in the club gettin' tipsy," the hook from Jermaine Dupri protégé J-Kwon's song "Tipsy," an infectious hit from the winter of 2004.

Before we arrived in Rio, Will told us that "Tipsy" was in his head because he'd heard it on the car ride to the airport. But after hearing him randomly bust out with "now everybody in the club gettin' tipsy" for three days straight, Will's initial declaration became suspect.

"Will, I'm beginning to think you really like that shit," said Tre, one of Will's former Howard buddies.

Then we all chimed in with our own thoughts on "Tipsy," shifting the discussion into a comparison of the current state of hip-hop with "back in the day," which for us meant the late '80s and early '90s.

The conversation was all over the place. One minute Tim, Will's best man, was lecturing us about Afrika Bambaataa, the Sugar Hill Gang, and Grandmaster Flash and the Furious Five. The next minute Jamel eulogized rapper Big L as he tinkered with his video camera. Then Ray, one of Will's friends from high school, yelled out "MC Hammer," broke out in the running man, and in mid-dance declared, "Don't front. Y'all niggas know you liked Hammer back in the day." Taking a pause, he added, "How many muthafuckas in here had a pair of Hammer pants? Raise your hands."

Getting up from his seat, Tim said, "Y'all niggas is crazy," then he walked out to the balcony to check on the rain, leaving the rest of us to laugh.

The conversation took yet another turn when Tre, slamming his hand on the coffee table in the center of the living room like a domino player throwing down the final bone in a victorious match, spoke out, "On the real. Greatest rapper of all time. Who you got?"

Not to be left playing the pack at his own party, Will slammed his own hand and announced, "Nah. Top five rappers of all time."

Ray leapfrogged into the center of the room, slammed down on the table, "I'm going to take a piss," turned around, and walked toward the bathroom cupping his crotch in an exaggerated b-boy gait.

After recovering from laughter, Tre conceded to Will's top-five request, "since it's his wedding," and started listing his top-five rappers:

5. Big Daddy Kane
4. Biggie
3. Tupac
2. Jay-Z

Taking a pause, Tre scanned the room, then shot out of his seat and said emphatically:

> "I'm a manifest and bless the mic I hold/
> You want it next? Then you gotta have
> soul" (Eric B. and Rakim, "I Know You
> Got Soul").

He didn't have to bother saying the name because that verse said it all; his nomination for the greatest rapper of all time was the legendary Rakim.

1. Rakim

For the next two hours each man rattled off his list and, following Tre's lead, capped off his litany with a sterling quote from his top-rated rapper's catalog.

There was very little variation. Jay-Z, Biggie, Tupac, and Rakim were on the top spots of pretty much everyone's lists. There were the occasional cameos by the likes of Common, Eminem, Ice Cube, and Juvenile. Will, whose list he said "changes like the weather," included Big Daddy Kane, Biggie, Kool G Rap, and Rakim, with Jay-Z at the head.

Jamel had arguably the most surprising list:

5. Biggie
4. Redman (Man does have a point. *Whut!*
    The Album is classic material)
3. Ghostface Killah
2. Raekwon
1. The Genius

However, for the most part, our lists didn't dramatically differ from Tre's. This probably explains why we all paid so much attention to our quotes. Since we couldn't outdo each other with a resounding list, guys sought magnanimous lines:

- "I'm the authentic poet to get lyrical/ And, stepping to me, yo that's the wrong move" (Big Daddy Kane, "Ain't No Half Steppin'").
- "Was born rough and rugged, addressin' the mad public/My attitude was, 'Fuck it,' 'cause motherfuckers love it" (Tupac, "Ambitionz az a Ridah").

Never being great at hip-hop quotables, I stayed true to the initial challenge and tried coming up with a list that blended Jamel's acknowledgment of less commercially successful lyricists with Tre's traditional murderers'-row lineup. I listed:

5. Scarface
4. Big Daddy Kane
3. Jay-Z
2. Rakim

All that I needed was a quote to announce my top rapper, but figuring that "They're jiggling baby; go head baby" or "Brenda's got a big ol' butt; I know I told you I'd be true" wouldn't impress any of these guys, I just announced his name:

1. LL Cool J

As soon as I said it, the man's name rang out through the apartment like a round of gunshots.

"LL Cool J?"

"LL Cool J?"

"LL Cool J?"

"Fo, all weekend I've been thinking that you were smart, but now I see you're just another crazy nigga," Ray shouted as he shook his head on his way out of the living room to take Tim's place on the balcony. "LL muthafuckin' Cool J."

For the first time in hours, Jamel, whose support I thought was guaranteed, put down his camera so that he could fully express his disgust. Looking me in the eyes as he pointed his right index finger at my chest, Jamel said, with a handful of disgust, "Y'all Queens niggas always gotta run together? Seriously, LL Cool J?" If he had known that Cool J and I went to the same middle school, albeit at different times, and that as a little kid my teachers often put him forth as a role model, Jamel would've been even more adamant in his position.

Doing my best to talk over the indignant shouts of "LL Cool J," I tried explaining that Cool J has to be the greatest because he's managed to remain relevant for over twenty years and has had hits in three decades. If it weren't for LL breaking through and starring in *Krush Groove*, there'd be no *8 Mile* or *Get Rich or Die Tryin'*, the biopics of rappers Eminem and 50 Cent, respectively.

No one paid attention to my argument. Moments ago we had all seemed too worn out to complete this lone conversation, but after my LL announcement there were about six different conversations taking place in the room that alternated between attempts at diagnosing my sanity to shouting matches over people's lists. Will, who appeared to be the most worn-out while lying on the couch with his legs splayed over one of the arms, suddenly shot out of his seat and spit: "LL Cool J is hard as hell/Battle anybody I don't care who you tell."

Will quieted the room. Although no one admitted it, once the conversation turned to "Rock the Bells," the song Will quoted, my assertion no longer seemed as farfetched.

"Rock the Bells" is a great song from a great rap album. Cool J's 1985 *Radio* also featured the classic cuts "I Can't Live Without My Radio," "I Need a Beat," and "Dear Yvette." *Radio* launched Cool J to the forefront of the rap world, which at the time was lorded over by the likes of Run-D.M.C., Kurtis Blow, and Grandmaster Flash, and established him as rap's first teen idol and sex symbol. The then pugnacious seventeen-year-old emcee cultivated a legion of female admirers because of his penchant for wearing Troop sweat suits with the jacket open to reveal his six-pack.

"Rock the Bells" features one of my all-time favorite Cool J stanzas. About three-quarters into the song, he takes aim at arguably the four biggest music stars of 1984 and '85. He asserts that Springsteen's glory days had passed, declares he has enough sexual prowess to relieve Madonna of her virginity, and suggests he's more popular than Michael Jackson and Prince. Never before had a rapper directed their freestyle-battle vitriol toward pop stars. In fact, while other rappers have lampooned less established pop artists such as Vanilla Ice and Milli Vanilli, no other rapper has yet to take shots at artists remotely approaching the stature of Springsteen, Madonna, Jackson, and Prince. This battle approach was characteristic of Cool J's—and in many ways rap's—early sound. It was the verbal equivalent to the bare drum-machine riffs and scratching also synonymous with mid-'80s hip-hop.

Radio was produced by Rick Rubin, the Def Jam co-founder who orchestrated the label's sound early on, infusing the records of Cool J and the Beastie Boys with a hard-rock edge similar to the jagged soundscape he later created for Jay-Z on "99 Problems" from 2003's *Black Album*. Recruiting Rubin to produce "99 Problems" was Jay-Z's way of paying homage to all of rap's early pioneers, and as he raps on his record, Jay-Z reminds us that rap's early battle style wasn't concocted solely for artists to attack one another. As with Cool J on "I Can't Live Without My Radio" and "Rock the Bells," Jay-Z's rhymes indicate that Rubin's razor-sharp beats are a powerful tool for unnerving the authority figures (e.g., music critics, apathetic adults, and police officers) trying to rein in artists.

Discussing "Rock the Bells" brought my pals and me back to comparing today's artists and those of yesteryear. This time, instead of trying to decide which generation was better, we tried compiling a list of contemporary versions of old-school artists. For example, Nas was Rakim. Jay-Z was Big Daddy Kane. Scarface was Kool G Rap. When we got to Cool J, we got stuck in a dispute between who made the better new LL, 50 Cent or Nelly? It seemed as if we were setting ourselves up for another marathon session when Ray, who had been surprisingly restrained for the last hour, called out from the balcony where he was smoking a cigar: "All you muthafuckas is wrong. LL Cool J is the new LL Cool J." And without saying another word, he turned back around to continue puffing on his cigar as he looked out over the Ipanema boardwalk. I don't think anyone knew whether or not to laugh because it wasn't clear if Ray was being serious or silly; but as I think our silence suggested, we at least knew he was right.

As was the case throughout that weekend, the silence didn't last long. Picking up his camera from the table to film Ray smoking on the balcony, Jamel called out, "Top five hip-hop film soundtracks of all time," as a mischievous grin ran across his face.

15. "FEELIN' ON YO BOOTY" AND "STEP IN THE NAME OF LOVE" /
R. Kelly

*We look for the sermon in the suicide, for the
social or moral lesson in the murder of five.*

—JOAN DIDION,
The White Album

When R. Kelly first appeared in 1992 as the lead singer of R. Kelly & Public Announcement, I thought that he and his bandmates were a poor imitation of Guy, the new jack swing trio fronted by Aaron Hall. As a New Yorker I came of age listening to Guy classics like "I Like" and "Groove Me," and was skeptical about any bands that I perceived to be biting their style. My skepticism was initially legitimated when R. Kelly and Public Announcement failed to achieve wide-ranging success with their debut album.

A year later, when Kelly released his solo effort, *12 Play*, it seemed as if Kelly was again biting Hall, who had left Guy and was on the verge of releasing his own solo LP in 1993, *The Truth*. This was getting to be ridiculous; not only were these two men shadowing each other careerwise, but Kelly and Hall were about the same complexion, had the same bald dome, were perpetually wearing sunglasses, and had powerful voices. But, shortly after the release of *12 Play* and "Bump n' Grind," "Your Body's Callin'," and "It Seems Like You're Ready" became part of everyday parlance, it was evident that these were two very different men, and that only one of them would go on to become the R&B maestro of his generation. The man who was once mistaken for Aaron Hall now has a legion of singers following in his footsteps—Jaheim, Case, Avant, Donell Jones, just to name a few—none of whom will ever be mistaken for the self-proclaimed "Pied Piper of R&B."*

I was never much of an R. Kelly fan except in the case of hits like "I Believe I Can Fly," which was featured in the movie *Space Jam*, and the rousing "The World's Greatest," which he recorded for the soundtrack of *Ali*. In my attempt at catering to highbrow musical tastes, I looked down on Kelly's light-hearted romps as scatological and unworthy of all the attention that he received. However, in 2000, when Kelly released his fifth album, *TP-2.Com*, I was drawn into his lair.

On his first single from *TP-2.Com*, "I Wish," Kelly updates Stevie Wonder's classic from *Songs in the Key of Life* that bears the same name.† Kelly's is an elegy for a deceased friend, while Wonder's is a recounting of the days that have passed away. Both of the scoundrels narrating these stories

* The legend of the Pied Piper is that, in the thirteenth century, he entranced the children of a village with his flute and locked them in a cave as a way of punishing the villagers for reneging on an earlier deal they'd made with him; it's an odd moniker to adopt, especially for an artist who's been plagued by some of the scandals that Kelly has.
† Rapper Will Smith also samples heavily from "I Wish" on his single "Wild Wild West" (*Willenium*, 1999). Smith's "Wild Wild West" was originally recorded as part of the soundtrack for his 1999 film of the same name.

right themselves as they mature into adulthood. Kelly has gone on to enjoy the fruits of his success while his childhood friend is no longer there to enjoy them with him. He appears to be casting this deceased friend as a metaphor for the simpler days that he enjoyed before becoming overwhelmed by the responsibilities of stardom.

Kelly's "I Wish" is all at once a testimonial to his friend, a declaration of Kelly's loyalty, and, lastly, a meditation on the trying conditions facing young black men. The range of emotional connections inspired by "I Wish" is completely divorced from the feelings inspired by another *TP-2.Com* track, "Feelin' on Yo Booty." In the same tradition as Al Green, Ronald Isley, and Prince, Kelly's voice transcends the boundaries between the sacred and the profane, eschewing the secular for the sexual. "Feelin' on Yo Booty" isn't Kelly's sexiest song, but it is sexy enough to give you an inside look into what one friend refers to as a person's "sexuary."

The track is a tongue-in-cheek come-on that doubles as a legitimate slow-dance song. In a musical era where radio-friendly amorous arrangements usually come in the form of hip-hop and R&B collaborations or teenage-geared ballads, the slow joint has virtually become a lost art. "Booty" is unequivocally adult and can only be appreciated by taking the time to slow down and indulge in its libidinousness.

Back in 2002, when I thought of myself as another one of the crooners helping bring the falsetto back, I sang "Booty" every chance I got. Usually I'd perform it for Tricia when she and her booty were within reach. She hated the song. She hated my affection for it even more. Yet she couldn't resist falling under its spell whenever we had a moment alone and I started singing its concluding hook, "BOO-OO-OH-TAY . . . BOO-OO-OOH-TAY."

It was worse when it came on the radio because I always sang along. It was safe to do this when we were alone. However, it was a totally different matter doing this in public. While Tricia and I were cruising through Atlanta's Little Five Points district with our friend Linda, "Booty" came on the radio in Linda's jeep. Tricia, knowing the danger that loomed, lunged for the radio to try switching the station. It was too late. The wolf had heard the howl of the leader of his pack, and I sang until Linda and Tricia were overcome with laughter.

"Feelin' on Yo Booty" really isn't much of a song. I don't mean that dismissively or as a critique, but "Booty" is a four-minute-long come-on, the dance-floor equivalent to pillow talk. One doesn't sing something like "Booty"; rather, you whisper it in your lover's ear as the two of you slow dance at the local club. Sung by any of his contemporaries (with the possible exception of D'Angelo) "Booty" would surely be a flop, a trite vanity exercise. Kelly manages to make it endearing. First there's the way that he sets the scene; it's easy to imagine him walking up to a woman and offering his lines. His voice captures the dank nature of club courtship where romance is spun through bold, "thugged out" directness, and where commitment rarely extends beyond the morning after.

In any other context the way that Kelly outlines the woman's body—"Now your body's got me feelin' like spending/With a backroom I could come to live in"—would merit a slap, but in the club and with both parties under the influence of an inebriating slow jam, it is more likely to make his lust interest blush. Kelly knows better than any other artist from the last fifteen years that people don't always feel like being patronized with flowery proclamations involving lush waterfalls. He understands that his listeners' fantasies often take place inside the bedroom and the club, and that his job as an artist is to create music to make those fantasies come true.

Still, don't be fooled by his "thugged out" role-playing. Kelly's talent is not born out of accident, reclamation, or hyperbolic "hustlin'." He was trained at Chicago's Kenwood High School, an institution known for its rigorous academics and creative-arts programs. Kelly's talent bears the marks of an individual reared for success rather than merely rescued from "the streets," a point that comes through in his arrangements that are equally mesmerizing in either their grandeur or their simplicity. He is a versatile songwriter capable of penning something as uplifting as "I Believe I Can Fly" or as frivolous as "Thoia Thong."

Kelly, true to his Pied Piper alter ego, has not adopted one pose, overly bound himself to commercialism, or positioned himself to attract a homogeneous following. (Remember the duet he did with Celine Dion, "I'm Your Angel"?) His lyrics are often as frail as they are strong, as repulsive as they are infectious, and his voice, that voice—he makes it an aqueduct to the soul as well as to the flesh.

I admired his range and versatility. But when something like pedophilia comes into play, as it did for Kelly in February 2002 when a video allegedly featuring him having sex with a minor was anonymously forwarded to the *Chicago Sun-Times*, I have to decide whether or not to abandon my growing reverence for the Pied Piper. The fact that Kelly hadn't been convicted (and as of this writing hasn't seen or done jail time) of this crime didn't matter, and, as I was reminded, everyone should have seen the signs of this happening when in 1994 reports surfaced that he had married his then-protégée, Aaliyah.

The controversy surrounding Kelly intensified when he had a falling out with rapper Jay-Z, with whom he had collaborated in 2002 on *The Best of Both Worlds*. The album supposedly faltered because of Kelly's unavailability to promote and perform at concerts as he dealt with the charges pending against him. For the first time in his public career, R & B's Teflon Don no longer seemed invincible. His struggles in the press and the courts kept him from doing what just two years earlier he seemed born to do—make great music.

Then in February 2003, a month after further accusations of child pornography were leveled against him, Kelly released *Chocolate Factory*. This album and the 2004 double-disc follow-up, *Happy People / U Saved Me*, was a paean to his Chicago roots and a return to the coquettish ballads that fueled his early success. In fact, the first few lines of the *Chocolate Factory* lead single, "Ignition," refer to the title of his 1995 hit "You Remind Me of Something."

I was dumbfounded that in the midst of all the controversy swirling around him, Kelly had the gall to release a song that coyly asks his paramour if he can put his "key" in her "ignition." The song, sounding as if it's intended for the BET 106 Park crowd (meaning young black music listeners), defied any explanation. Was he that bold?

However, the more that I listened to "Ignition (Remix)," the harder it became to deny its merits. Lyrically Kelly has a knack for blending bad-boy poetics with the traditional

R&B romantic balladeer proclamations. Comparing women to cars is normally an unpoetic maneuver by those lacking in imagination, yet somehow Kelly makes it sound alluring. I think it's because he learned early on how to sing like a rapper. On "Ignition (Remix)" he name-drops all the materialistic status symbols—Lexus Coupes, Navigator Jeeps, and Cristal champagne—that by the late '90s had become staples of the rap lexicon.

One gets the sense that Kelly's world is alternately nihilistic, playfully erotic, and—as is the case of "Step in the Name of Love," another track on *Chocolate Factory*—a living homage to his elders and his native Chicago.

My most memorable encounter with "Step in the Name of Love" came in the fall of 2003. I had gone to a fundraiser for a youth group in New York and as I waited for my friend, "Step in the Name of Love" came over the speakers. This was during the high point of the R. Kelly boycott instituted by my self-righteous black bohemian friends and me, so when my date (at least I think she was my date), a recent transplant from Chicago, leapt up and pulled me to dance with her when the song came on, I froze. Do I dance with her and let things take their course, or do I try to dissuade her? I opted for the latter, whispering in her ear, "We're boycotting R. Kelly."

She was intent on getting me to dance with her so she disregarded my objections and led me back out to the dance floor where we'd spent the better half of the last three hours. Having only seen step dancing during the first-date sequence in the movie *Love Jones*, I didn't have the faintest idea of how to step. Thanks to some coaching courtesy of my Chi lady, within moments I had learned the basics.

In many ways "Step in the Name of Love" is the antithesis of "Ignition." It's a laid-back groove in the vein of the Philly soul sound orchestrated by Philadelphia International masterminds Kenny Gamble and Leon Huff. While "Ignition" promotes materialism, compares women to cars, and offers lyrics that you hope the children in the room can't decipher, "Step in the Name of Love" is an homage to one of the finer art forms of Kelly's Chicago, one to which any parent would be proud to introduce their child. Stepping is to black Chicagoans what the tango is to Argentineans, a six- to eight-count social dance that puts a premium on partnering, spins, and fanciful footwork. Stepping parties often attract mature audiences because the music played during stepping parties is remixed versions of '70s and '80s soul classics. However, after the release of Kelly's *Chocolate Factory* and *Happy People/U Saved Me*, these parties experienced an influx of younger participants. The Pied Piper's success in regenerating interest in stepping proved that he doesn't always have to cater his music to younger audiences in order for them to follow him.

Kelly, who has long made his reification of Ronald Isley and the Isley Brothers clear, uses "Step in the Name of Love" to show his appreciation for Chicago legends Regina and George Daniels, owners of George's Music Room, a well-known record store on the city's West Side. He also thanks Donnie Lyle, a guitarist who appears on many of his albums, as well as Wayne Williams, renowned Chicago dance deejay and longtime Kelly collaborator who co-produced "Step in the Name of Love" and the other "steppers' anthems" on *Happy People/U Saved Me*. Kelly underscores his appreciation for the gifts that his native city has provided him with a litany of thank-yous at the end of "Step in the Name of Love." Here we get a humbler Kelly, a man seemingly conscious of the gravity of the allegations swirling around him, unlike the one filled with hubris found singing on "Ignition."

Kelly carries the community-oriented focus of "Step in the Name of Love" on to its video. He bypasses the traditional bevy of video vixens and athletic-jersey and Timbs-wearing compatriots for a collage of Chicago steppers, young and old, balding men and heavyset women. In other words, the types of black folks that contemporary image-conscious R&B artists have long forgotten. The shots of the middle-aged and twentysomething couples decked out all in white stepping across the dance floor shows the earnestness of Kelly's vision, his love for the people of Chicago and their graceful art form, and the organic nature of the reverie espoused by a song like "Step in the Name of Love."

The Pied Piper moniker and his video opera *Trapped in the Closet* are only two of the displays of Kelly's eccentric nature. These unconventional habits detract from his talent as a singer and composer, and suggest that like many other musicians, talent and success in the form of public adulation aren't enough for Kelly. He must find other ways to push boundaries. He strives to reveal to his listeners that he is wrestling with forces, maybe even demons, far greater than any we could imagine. With his peculiar behavior and allegations of criminal misconduct with minors, Kelly, like legends before him—Jimi Hendrix, Marvin Gaye, and, more recently, Kurt Cobain—keeps me looking "for the sermon in the suicide, for the social or moral lesson in the murder of five."

16. "JESUS WALKS" / *Kanye West*

I am proud to say that I was raised in "the church." My church rearing, at least the United States portion of it, began with Saturday-morning Bible studies in the corridors of Blessed Virgin Mary Church in Jamaica, Queens. Later I became a member and then a mentor in Immaculate Conception's teen club. The Monday evenings spent facilitating discussions in this Jamaica Estates church were ideal practice runs for my eventual career as a college professor. On Immaculate's campus I had some of my first spirited conversations about religion, the meaning and presence of God in a person's life, and the difference between sinning and being human. I also met my first love at Immaculate and had my first adult relationship, or at least as adult as one could have as a college freshman.

Just as I used to spend Monday nights in one of Immaculate's studies with my peers when I was in high school and college, I now spend Friday evenings in the parlors of Brooklyn's Emmanuel Baptist Church fellowshipping with other adults, trying to find answers to many of the issues that I grapple with—most notably finding love, locating our purpose and place within our chosen professions at such early stages in our careers, and building and nurturing meaningful relationships with other Christians.

As much as I have benefited from experiences like those at Immaculate and Emmanuel, they sometimes can be overwhelming, especially for a person such as myself who's a bit of an eccentric and engages in practices, most notably premarital sex, that many Christians frown upon. During various sessions at Immaculate or Emmanuel I often found myself wondering: Aren't my sins measures of my humanity? Should I feel guilty about them? Why should any of my pronouncements send anyone else scurrying for his or her Bible? Am I a "good Christian"?

I have spent many an evening wondering whether I am wrong for enjoying things that might cause some of my Christian brothers and sisters to go down on their knees praying for my soul. At times I have been extremely self-conscious about how my peers would regard my affinity for long nights at the club, my faith that a person can believe in both God and the gods, and that liturgical dancing is a legitimate form of foreplay.

As I sit here with an iPod in one hand and a Bible in the other, reflecting on my spiritual walk, I find myself fondly venturing back to when Kanye West issued *The College Dropout*. West exploded onto the scene and announced to the world that "Jesus Walks," and brought into the secular, sometimes profane, environment of hip-hop clubs the art of praising Christ. West's "Jesus Walks" took the work that Kirk Franklin began with "Why We Sing"—to make gospel and Christianity more palatable to younger audiences—combined it with an unparalleled intellectual funk sound reminiscent of Chicago legend Curtis Mayfield, and gave the hip-hop audience a gospel anthem in our own language with curses and all. West proved to the world that while he may be a college dropout, he surely isn't a Christian dropout.

Prior to "Jesus Walks," I didn't pay any attention to hip-hop gospel music. Okay, in all honesty I still don't pay attention to hip-hop gospel music. I don't like gospel rap for the same reason that I have heard many people, including some fundamentalist Christians, give for ignoring "secular" rap music—all of the hip-hop gospel I've heard pretty much sounds alike. Some of these songs have the outdated feel of mid-'80s R&B and rap collaborations where established R&B artists placed random or, rather, unknown "rappers" on their records in an attempt to reach a younger audience.

I haven't found a gospel rap artist whose music is compelling enough for me to remember. The good Christian in me feels obliged to say that these praise anthems and recurring tales of being wayward and then found are better for humanity than the rampant materialism and violence that permeates a lot of "secular" rap music. However, the good human in me knows that there's nothing like experiencing the delirium in a hip-hop club when something like DMX's "Get at Me Dog" comes on. Once, as my brother and I walked down Thirty-fourth Street in Manhattan with friends late one night after taking part in some of the festivities for the 1998 NBA All-Star weekend, a caravan of cars drove by blasting "Get at Me Dog." When DMX started barking, my brother and I, our friends, and half the people on the street barked right back at him.

I have a similar visceral response to "Jesus Walks." I respond to West's call with the same fervor that I would to one of Luke's chants on a 2 Live Crew record or DMX's bark. I nod my head to Kanye's rhymes and raise my right arm in the air to testify to the spirit transforming my favorite rapper into my favorite preacher as I am transported from Club 112 to Emmanuel Baptist Church. I am taken in by the powerful image that West invokes of Jesus walking. West has remixed the traditional gospel axiom of "There's a sweet spirit in our midst" into a hip-hop processional fit for both the street and the sanctuary.

"Jesus Walks" tells the tale of a person whose soul is susceptible to being compromised by the "devil" and all of the societal ills that this spirit endows: materialism, greed, murder, drugs, and racism. Through his convictions and faith in Jesus, West manages to overcome the diabolical spirits preying on his soul. He then feels compelled to testify about his experience despite the fact that by doing so he risks losing all of the worldly possessions that many other rap artists laud: money, cars, jewelry, and fame.

West drew the ire of Christians and conservative pundits when he appeared as Christ for the cover of the February 9, 2006, issue of *Rolling Stone*. Along with the controversy, the photo fueled interest in West's 2005 album, *Late Registration*.

Unlike West's musical creations, neither the picture nor the controversy swirling around its publication was a new revelation in rap circles. West was simply the latest in a slew of rappers who have donned a similar guise. Before West, there was Tupac Shakur, whose first posthumous album, *The Don Killuminati: The 7 Day Theory* (1996), featured a graphic of him hanging on a cross. Three years later, rappers Nas and Sean "Puff Daddy" Combs resurrected this image when they were both depicted being crucified in the video for their collaboration "Hate Me Now." (Combs later fought to have his scene removed from the video.) Then, of course, there's Jay-Z, who counts "Jay-Hova" among his many appellations.

No matter how profane many people would like to accuse rappers of being, we must acknowledge that they often draw their inspiration from biblical figures. And of course, since rappers are obsessed with crowning themselves kings of New York, the South, or wherever else, and the overwhelming majority of popular rappers are male, it makes sense that they'd also want to capture one of the most esteemed thrones in the Bible. This is further compounded by the fact that as black men, many of these rappers grew up idolizing men like Malcolm X and Martin Luther King Jr., whose lives were cut short before they could fulfill their destinies as the "black Moses." In a peculiar way, it seems that oftentimes we men are trying to do with the Bible what we once did with comic books and action figures.

To his credit, on "Jesus Walks," West is not suggesting that he is Jesus. He appeals for his salvation, as well as that of others, but doesn't imply that he can accomplish this himself. However, from my time spent in churches I wonder if it's salvation that we are searching for—or have we conflated salvation with definition? What I believe many people, or should I say, *I* am often looking for in my time in church is definition, a way of understanding my life. Much of this definition has come from what I have been taught as a Christian about Jesus, but I'd be lying if I were to say that biblical figures and Holy Rollers are the only ones influencing my life. I've been shaped by my time observing the practices of my priests and pastors as much as I have by time spent hanging with friends who made the streets their home.

Moreover, as Chicago rapper Common pronounces on his anthem "G.O.D. (Gaining One's Definition)":

> *My mind had dealt with the books of Zen, Tao the lessons*
> *Koran and the Bible, to me they all vital . . .*

I happily pronounce that Jesus walked, yet I also know that he is not the only Supreme Being marshaling the human procession through this universe. True, salvation is a key Christian concept, but it's the struggle to gain one's definition that is actually the vital force uniting us all as humans.

17. "BILLS, BILLS, BILLS" AND "INDEPENDENT WOMEN" /
Destiny's Child

One day while walking past some of the row houses that dot Prospect Place in Brooklyn, where I live, I heard this group of late-teen/early twentysomethings talking about music. Their conversation piqued my interest because ever since I started writing *Songs in the Key of My Life*, whenever I heard people talking about music, I listened to see if they were talking about any of the songs discussed in the book. There were eight people in their crew: six men and two women. The five guys in the thick of the conversation talked with their arms as if they were jousting over each point. A girl completed the hexagon they had formed, trying her best to finish her point. The last guy was resting against a fence by the park while embracing his girlfriend. Their lips were close, eager to consummate a pending kiss that was perpetually interrupted by a smile or giggle brought about by the string of wisecracks being made by the others.

I walked upon them slowly taking this all in, standing on the periphery for a moment. And just as I was about to pass through their sphere one of the guys said the sentence that would stay with me for the duration of the summer of 2005: "Destiny's Child started that feminist shit with that song 'Bills, Bills, Bills' and that other joint . . ." He flailed his right arm as he tried to come up with the name. The guy making out in the corner with his girlfriend called out, " 'Independent Women.' "

" 'Bills, Bills, Bills'? Isn't that the song where they're asking dudes to pay their bills?" I thought. "Last time I checked there was nothing feminist about a woman being dependent on a man. So what's he talking about?"

It took me a few months and dozens of conversations with friends about this incident to realize that the guy was right, sort of. "Bills, Bills, Bills" is actually a feminist-ish song. If I had really listened to the song rather than just pooh-pooh it, like many other listeners back in 1999, I might've realized this sooner.

When *The Writing's on the Wall*, the album on which "Bills" appears, was released, I was in my first year of graduate school. In my mind, I had outgrown Destiny's Child. Their music was too high-schoolish and was best left for my brother and his friends.

On "Bills" the women of Destiny's Child (which at that time consisted of Beyoncé Knowles, LeToya Luckett, La-Tavia Roberson, and Kelendria "Kelly" Rowland) voice their displeasure with men who are trying to take advantage of their success. In the first and second verses, they detail how they're fed up with leeches who're more interested in siphoning women's earnings than working for their own. When I first heard "Bills," I paid more attention to the hook "Can you pay my bills?" than I did to the song's larger story. I misguidedly denounced them as materialistic, moneygrubbing gold diggers.

One reason for this confusion was the similarities between "Bills, Bills, Bills" and "No Scrubs," a hit single by the group TLC that was released prior to "Bills, Bills, Bills," in 1999. Both selections were composed by the husband-and-wife duo of producer Kevin "She'kspere" Briggs and songwriter Kandi Burrus, formerly of the group Xscape. "Bills, Bills, Bills" and "No Scrubs" rely on a similar mix of drum and keyboard instrumentals and comparable refrains. However, they are very dissimilar in terms of content; while "No Scrubs" accuses men of being scrubs because, among other things, they don't have a car, live with their mothers, and don't have the money to take their women on trips across the globe, "Bills, Bills, Bills" specifically deals with men who take advantage of their ladies. Destiny's Child does refer to these men as "scrubs," but they place more emphasis on how men are unfairly compromising their relationships.

If you didn't get the message with "Bills, Bills, Bills," on "Independent Women" Destiny's Child (which by now had become the trio of Knowles, Rowland, and Michelle Williams) reprises their role as pop music's reigning black feminist voices. This fast-paced single was originally recorded for the soundtrack of the motion picture *Charlie's Angels*, and appears on their 2001 album, *Survivor*. After the ladies identify some of their notable material possessions—diamond rings, houses, and cars—they follow these allusions with the refrain "I've bought it," the emphasis being on their ability to pay for these items themselves. They realize that the onus for achieving happiness and success is on them and not on others, just as it is when it comes to acquiring their possessions. They are encouraging women to celebrate their ability to depend on themselves, a point brought to life by the upbeat melody-line fusion of thunderclap drums and synth violin riffs.

A few months after that incident on the block, I was invited to give a talk for Black History Month at Dartmouth College. In preparation, I asked some of my students at Eugene Lang College in New York what kind of Black History Month presentation they would like to hear if given the option. I threw a topic out there, partly in jest, to gauge their interest. One of the women in the class immediately leaped to affirm that there was some merit to the young man's statement. She argued that while "Destiny's Child didn't start that feminist-ish," they were part of what some call the third wave, or third generation, of feminists. A male student at the table argued just as passionately that he found the statement "dubious," because when he thinks of black feminists he thinks of "Angela Davis, Alice Walker, and Nikki Giovanni, not Destiny's Child." The woman shot back that Destiny's Child could be still considered feminist vocalists because "Bills" and "Independent Women" focus on women's experiences and on women empowering themselves, not on bashing men.

Their visceral reactions to the talk's title, "Destiny's Child Started That Feminist-Ish," convinced me that I had found the subject of my talk. I'd intended for the talk to be a repudiation of the comment heard on the street; instead, it evolved into a broader discussion about African American feminism and its relationship to black history in general. I thought I'd be playing teacher, but the spirited intellectual debates that ensued once the students at Lang, and later at Dartmouth, heard the topic provided me with a welcome opportunity to be a student, bringing me right back to where I started that day on the street.

At Dartmouth's Cutter Shabazz House in February 2006, after politely listening to me offer my brief summary of black feminism and black history, the students there repeated many of the Lang students' points almost verbatim. They then talked about feminism in rap music, making references to the lyrics of rappers Foxy Brown, Lil' Kim, and Remy Ma with the same ease that they quoted scholars bell hooks, Chandra Mohanty, and Tricia Rose.

Looking at the brown and black faces in that room I realized that this talk was an opportunity to bring together their knowledge gleaned from the streets with what they were acquiring in the classroom. I discovered that these students, all of whom were about a year or two younger than my brother, did more than simply ogle the clothes and bodies of artists like Destiny's Child. They also listened.

After the talk at Dartmouth, I had dinner with three of the faculty and staff members in attendance. All of us were thirty years of age or older, meaning that none of us were in high school when "Bills, Bills, Bills" and "Independent Women" were released. As we went around the room sharing our thoughts on the conversation that just took place, each person admitted that they had to go back and listen to these songs again.

A few months later, Renee, a friend who teaches at another college in the Northeast, confessed, "It's now fair to say that I'm obsessed with Beyoncé, whose CD keeps me constant company up here. I've gone as far as to contemplate teaching her in my black feminism course in the spring."

18. "YOU'RE SO VAIN" / *Carly Simon*

Devoid of a clear view of the stars, the New York skyline functioned as a fine substitute as Delia and I sat in each other's arms on my roof on a cool late-August evening in 2005. We giggled at my declaration that the Empire State Building's lights were red, black, and green that night in honor of Marcus Garvey. We marveled at the planes circling overhead as they waited to descend into one of the two New York–area airports. Most of all we kissed, arms embracing each other's backs as our hands roamed for spaces allowing access to the flesh that lay beneath our clothing. These kisses and hugs were the only way we knew how to keep warm that didn't involve one of us going back downstairs for a blanket or jacket. Our smooching was the best way to circumvent our absence from each other, even if it were only a momentary one, becoming interludes in a conversation about nothing in particular that neither of us wanted to end for one reason in particular, love. Somehow we started talking about *Songs in the Key of My Life*. My talking must've caused too long of an intermission between the next set of kisses. Delia tried pulling me into a kiss, letting out a growl, her signal that she was restless. I wanted to finish my point, so she let go of my neck and her pursuit of another kiss. Then she said, "Are you going to add that Carly Simon song?"

"What Carly Simon song?"

"You gotta have that song," she pressed on as a smirk blossomed.

"What Carly Simon song?"

Her smirk had become full-out laughter. " 'You're So Vain,' " she declared as she fell back on the ground and pulled me down with her.

The more that *I* tried explaining how *I* could not put "You're So Vain" in the book because *I* did not have a personal connection to it, that *I* did not have a story with which *I* could connect to it, and how *I* need to always remember that each song must have a clear connection to *my life*, the more Delia's laughter intensified.

"I can't believe it," she shouted, "you're so fucking vain."

"What?" I shrugged in bewilderment.

"It's the truth. I can't believe it. You're so fucking vain."

I disagreed. Yet, I eventually had a story to tell about Simon's song.

"You're So Vain" is an amusing dressing-down of an unnamed lover from Simon's 1972 album *No Secrets*. Part of the reason for the song's initial popularity was the speculation that it fueled as listeners sought to discern which one of her superstar lovers Simon was crooning about. Was it husband James Taylor? On the other hand, was she referring to one of her former beaus, Warren Beatty or Mick Jagger? Simon has never publicly disclosed who was the inspiration for this song, choosing instead to further whet her fans' appetites by saying that "You're So Vain" refers to a composite of men she encountered during her time in Los Angeles in the late '60s and early '70s.

Lyrically it's one of the most ingenious songs I've ever heard. Each stanza is a story unto itself, which makes me believe Simon's statement that this song is about a group of men rather than one individual. The escapades that she narrates this character getting involved in are all at once absurd (hanging out with stealthy spies) and sublime (flying on a whim to Nova Scotia to see the eclipse). He sounds more like a James Bond clone than a real-life dude. His ethereal dashing persona infuses the song with an air of fantasy that makes her crush on him more understandable.

However, since the song is not about him, and it's in fact about her feelings for him, his awe-inspiring antics are negated by her remorse over having met him. Simon brilliantly relays this feeling in these two powerful lines:

> But you gave away the things you loved
> And one of them was me . . .

These lyrics strike a chord every time that I hear them because of the equally moving lines that follow them about her dreams being clouds in her coffee. She says this so matter-of-factly that I found myself rewinding the song repeatedly to make sure I heard her correctly the first time. I'd be hard-pressed to find lyrics that more succinctly describe the feeling of being dumped than the ones offered by Simon.

The lines that I have quoted make "Vain" sound depressing, when it isn't. Simon sings in a fairly upbeat tone and her lyrics are so keen, woven together so intricately, that I have found myself marveling at this song more than anything else.

But I guess since this book is partly about me, and this song is about me and Delia, I must also confess that I feel uncomfortable associating this song with her because, well, I broke up with her. Despite how much I love her, and how well we seem to function as friends and during dating spurts, I never comfortably settled in to our relationship. I generally put work ahead of her and—as she often pointed out—ahead of the family and friends with whom I moped about not having closer connections to.

Around the same time that Delia prompted me to look into Simon's "You're So Vain," I was also obsessed with the book of Ecclesiastes, which is a sermon on the "vanity of vanities." One of the many passages that I was drawn to was this one from the eleventh verse in chapter two:

> Then I looked on all the works that my hands had wrought, and on the labour that I had laboured to do: and, behold, all *was* vanity and vexation of spirit, and *there was* no profit under the sun.

The preacher being quoted is warning his flock about the emptiness that comes from pursuing one thing over all others, and the verse captures the rest of the book's sentiments.

Months later, on a whim, I sat down and listened to Simon's "You're So Vain" again to see if I actually had a strong enough connection to it to write about it. That's when I saw the connection between "You're so Vain," Ecclesiastes, and myself. As Simon recounted her experiences with the gallivanting scoundrels of Los Angeles, I realized that the story was in fact very familiar. I was vain. And Delia wasn't around to share this epiphany. There was indeed no profit under the sun.

19. **"REAL LOVE"** / *Mary J. Blige*

Hail Mary, full of grace, the Lord is with thee;
blessed art thou among women.   —HAIL MARY

During my thirtieth birthday party in 2006, the deejay stopped spinning records and turned the stage over to my friends so that they could start singing karaoke. I braced myself for the worst. A karaoke catalog left in the wrong hands is a dangerous thing, and there are plenty of wrong hands in my circle of friends. My hands were probably the wrongest of them all when I got onstage and did a duet of Wyclef Jean and Mary J. Blige's "911" with my friend Tamala. Tamala, who actually has some vocal chops, carried our duo, while I sang an already off-key Wyclef even further off-key.

The other folks in attendance really bought into it, though; a troupe of friends got the party going by leading everyone in a chorus of Stevie Wonder's "Happy Birthday." Rick James's spirit was invoked surprisingly well by my friend Patrick, who did a rousing rendition of "Super Freak," backup dancer and all. And everyone loved it when two of the ladies from my church did Bell Biv DeVoe's "Poison." "Oh my," I said to myself and blushed as Natasha and Karen gave their booties a little smack as they belted out, "Never trust a big butt and a smile, that girl is . . . *Po-oizzzooonnnnnnnn*." The song that really brought the house down, though, was Mary J. Blige's "Real Love."

I know the whole purpose of karaoke is for people to sing along, but this was different. It wasn't just the person onstage, Tamala, or those in the front row singing along. Every person in the lounge was singing.

My friend Deidre was leaving, and as we said our good-byes, I heard extremely familiar drum taps. Deidre and I instantly turned our attention toward the stage. As Tamala sang, Deidre and I became swept up in the sea change occurring around us where one by one the gaggle of conversations about work, church, and the party petered out, morphing into a chorale rendition of "Real Love."

If you were from another planet, you'd be forgiven for thinking we were singing a national anthem or a sacred religious song. Although in a sense if you're a woman of a certain age and demographic, Blige's "Real Love" is exactly that. Black females born between 1970 and 1980 make up a large portion of this religion's demographic. Look longer and you'll notice that other parishioners include Latinas, Asians, Germans and other Europeans, young and old, all of whom wave their invisible rosaries in the air as they recite one of the homilies offered up by R&B's matron saint Mary. Listen closer and you'll hear some male baritones. Some are courageous enough to sing out loud. Others of us whisper lines beneath our breath like Catholic schoolboys reciting the act of contrition. But if the deejay switches over from the original to the "Real Love" remix on which producer Sean "P. Diddy" Combs ingeniously placed rapper Biggie Smalls, the male voices in the room become as audible as, if not louder than, the ladies'.

When Mary J. Blige burst on the scene in 1992 with *What's the 411?*, she was hailed as the next Chaka Khan or Aretha Franklin, the rap generation's Etta James or Billie Holiday. As her career progressed, she drew comparisons to Nina Simone and Bessie Smith. In other words, Blige was compared to virtually every major African American soul, blues, and R&B artist of the twentieth century, especially those whose personal stories flirted with tragedy. A decade later, in 2003, Blige was still generating analogies at the pace of an LSAT review instructor when her eighth album, *Love and Life*, debuted. Instead of comparisons to artists of yesteryear, Blige was now the multiplatinum standard against whom a whole slew of new female artists were being measured. Hip-hop and R&B ingenues like Ashanti, Keyshia Cole, and Amerie were being lauded as the next Mary J. Blige, the princesses of hip-hop and R&B. Even one of Blige's contemporaries, Faith Evans, was still struggling to escape Blige's shadow despite Evans's large fan base.

Unlike her male rapper peers who are continually vying for the title of king of hip-hop, king of New York, Blige's reign has been undisputed. "Real Love" was one of five highlights from *What's the 411?*: "Reminisce," "You Remind Me," "Sweet Thing," and the title track, "What's the 411?," a duet with rapper Grand Puba. Grand Puba, reveling in the success of his own 1992 album, *Reel to Reel*, which featured the classic "360 Degrees (What Goes Around)," was one of the standout contributors enlisted by Blige's then Svengali Combs. Other participants on the album included K-Ci Hailey, lead singer of the R&B troupe Jodeci and Blige's boo at the time, who collaborated with her on "I Don't Want to Do Anything." (Hailey's fellow Jodeci mate De-Vante Swing was also the song's co-producer.)

Meanwhile, "Real Love" was co-produced by the seemingly unlikely duo of Mark Morales and L.A. Reid. Reid eventually went on to replace the legendary Clive Davis as CEO of Arista Records before moving to the same post at Island Def Jam music group. Morales, formerly known as Prince Markie Dee of the Fat Boys, the corpulent late-'80s rap trio, worked as a producer with some of the most successful artists of the '90s, including Lisa Stansfield and Mariah Carey.

Morales and Reid provide Blige with a tableau for her to display gentler, more upbeat vocals without backing away from her hip-hop soul persona. Instead of a street-smart woman, Blige sounds like a teenage girl praying to be swept away by all that love has to offer, praying that the love she has been pining for is "real." The feeling of youthful innocence, of outlining a dream, is the tune's charm. "Real Love" is a song that sounds like its subject. It lacks hubris, ego, and melodrama and is sincere throughout—just like one imagines real love to be.

When "Real Love" came on during my party, all attendees uncorked any remaining vestiges of shyness or self-consciousness that had kept them from becoming fully immersed in the singathon. When Blige belts out that she's "searching for a real love," I take it to mean that she is in search of her liberation. She doesn't want the love from another human being who could possibly constrain her—the types of love she's already experienced. Instead, she wants the love, the liberation, that will unlock all her possibilities. Blige appeals for a love that is found within, which probably explains why everyone in that bar sang along with Blige as if their lives depended on it.

20. "IF IT MAKES YOU HAPPY" /
Sheryl Crow

My flight to Los Angeles in June 2006 began with an hour and a half's delay on the runway. I grew more anxious with each passing second, afraid that this holdup would surpass the five-hour delay that left some friends stranded on the JFK airport tarmac in June 2000. Fortunately for them, they had each other to swap tales with and share in the misery. Meanwhile I was traveling alone, my neighbor was asleep, and my nerves were too racked to try reading one of the books I'd brought.

A little over an hour into the delay, the woman sitting next to me woke up. She was very alarmed that we were still on the ground. One fist was clenched on her lap, tapping her jittery knee back down each time that it popped up. The other fist appeared on the verge of crushing the cell phone it was cradling as she stabbed numbers into it. Maybe I'd been watching too many episodes of the TV show *Entourage*, but I imagined that she was a Hollywood power broker, and when she put the phone to her ear, I braced myself to hear her chewing out her assistant for sticking her in coach. Better yet, she was going to apologize to Brad and Angelina for missing Maddox's birthday party.

Instead of screaming at someone, she calmly whispered into the phone, "Honey, my flight is delayed. Tell the kids I love them and can't wait for my hugs." Noticing me staring at her, she revealed that she has a flight phobia and takes medication which normally allows her to sleep during take-off and sometimes, depending on where she's flying, the entire trip. She then draped her blanket over her head and tried going back to sleep.

When she peeked out from beneath the blanket, I tried doing for her what others have done for me during turbulent flights: I talked to her. First, I confessed my own flying anxiety and told her about how I never sit by the window, relish sleeping through the duration of a flight, and if there happens to be any turbulence, my hands are guaranteed to leave an imprint in the armrests. Then I tried the usual light banter about where we lived, what we did for a living, exchanged names and the reasons for our respective trips. Diana seemed excited when I mentioned writing *Songs in the Key of My Life*, and offered the most intriguing response that anyone has ever given after hearing about the project: "My friend *would've* loved your book."

She went straight to talking about her friend and didn't stop. I was confused when Diana kept on referring to this friend in the past tense. As Diana and I continued talking, she eventually revealed that her friend, Lee, passed away five years ago after a battle with cancer. After taking a long look at me, Diana said Lee was about my age when she passed away. Lee had such a profound influence on Diana that every year, Diana celebrates her birthday by volunteering at a local charity, making a birthday cake in her honor with candles and all the trimmings, and, most important, playing Lee's favorite song, Sheryl Crow's "If It Makes You Happy."

Within minutes, Diana had gone from having a somewhat muted, anxious disposition to being very animated. Her hands were liberated from her lap and were now moving freely as she used them to frame imaginary portraits of her friend, who loved music and the outdoors and was the linchpin in their circle of friends due to her effervescent personality, which made her a joy to be around. Diana was now using her hands as borders for pictures of the cakes that she made every year, outlining the magnanimity that her friend personified and that has inspired Diana to continue having a positive impact on the lives of people she encounters.

Right before falling back asleep, when she couldn't ward off the power of her medication any longer, Diana reminded me for the umpteenth time: "Sheryl Crow's 'If It Makes You Happy,' go home and listen to it."

When we arrived in Los Angeles, Diana awoke from her nap and quickly exited the aircraft so that she could make her transfer to San Diego. She reminded me again to listen to Crow while retrieving her belongings from the overhead compartment. I wanted her to talk about Lee some more, but obviously time didn't allow for that. Most of all I wanted to find out more about what "If It Makes You Happy" meant to Diana, and why she was so comfortable telling me Lee's story and why she became so calm when doing so.

Back in the mid-1990s when a new crop of women singer/songwriters led by Tori Amos, Sheryl Crow, Sarah McLachlan, Alanis Morissette, and Liz Phair began gaining prominence I was more focused on the trials and tribulations of three New York–area rappers—Jay-Z, Nasty Nas, and Biggie. My pop-folk music collection was in need of serious updating since it had yet to progress past Suzanne Vega's first album and the soulful stirrings of Sinead O'Connor. When I finally got hip to the scene I invested my fortune in the career of Paula Cole, whose "I Don't Want to Wait" was the theme for *Dawson's Creek*, a show that I watched religiously during its first two seasons.

Except for feigning interest in Morissette and Crow to impress a woman I dated in the fall of 2003, Crow was an afterthought. I knew that she had won a slew of Grammys, but in truth, I knew more about her relationship with cyclist Lance Armstrong than I did about her music. I wasn't sure that I had ever heard a Sheryl Crow song.

As I peered through her catalog while downloading "If It Makes You Happy," I realized that I did know Crow's music, and enjoyed her work enough to have a Sheryl Crow top four, a list that turned to a top five after hearing "If It Makes You Happy." They are "Everyday Is a Winding Road," "Steve McQueen," "All I Wanna Do," and "Soak Up the Sun." I currently rank "If It Makes You Happy" fifth because it's the one with which I am least familiar. However, it continues climbing my newly minted Crow chart each time I hear it.

The first thing that jumped out was how Crow's biography was the quintessential tale of a person determined to make their dreams come true. She toiled in the background of the music industry for more than a decade before garnering international acclaim. She's written for Eric Clapton and Celine Dion, and has sung backup for Don Henley, Rod Stewart, Sting, Michael Jackson, and, lo and behold, Stevie Wonder. The connection to Wonder made me feel as if I was fated to meet Diana and write about Crow.

Coincidences aside, I truly appreciate Crow's talent as a songwriter. She has an inestimable talent for refrains that listeners can home in on as we try following her often eclectic verses. Usually an offering of folksy wisdom, these simple refrains are em dashes bringing to a halt the elaborate tales relayed by Crow in her songs. The hooks magnify the simple answers to life's befuddling riddles.

As she tells the tale of a wandering soul grappling with the ebbs and flows of life on "If It Makes You Happy," Crow offers this simple solution: "If it makes you happy, it can't be that bad." This effortless approach to dealing with dilemmas reveals itself in her ability to be self-deprecating, venture off on her free-verse lyrical jaunts, and focus on her own enjoyment rather than settling any vendettas or righting any wrongs. The sagacious folk wisdom she's dispensing is almost like a self-help book or Dr. Phil set to music, because what she's essentially saying is "Get over yourself."

Sheryl Crow, which won a Grammy for both Best Rock Album and Album of the Year, confirmed that Crow had established herself as a major artist, producing a successful second album after losing her trusted team of producers and dealing with the death of Kevin Gilbert, the close friend and ex-boyfriend who introduced her to the band Tuesday Night Music Club. Crow has also survived breast cancer, two bouts with depression, and the end of her public relationship with Armstrong.

Yet what I appreciate more than Crow's resolve is her embrace of an optimistic, free-flowing approach to life. As she instructs on "Everyday Is a Winding Road":

> *Lay back, enjoy the show*
> *Everybody gets high, everybody gets low . . .*

The optimism that Crow conveys on "Everyday Is a Winding Road" and "If It Makes You Happy" is inspirational and instructive. I've happily noticed that she hasn't used her songs as forums for exacting revenge on her former partners. She uses her music as a medium through which she can introspectively thresh for insight into problems.

Meditating on Crow's lyricism was a helpful exercise because her songs showed me another way of writing about life. Her upbeat lyrics brought home the lessons that my editor had been trying to impart for months; I don't need to overload my stories with sadness in order for readers to understand my pain, and there's a difference between feeling pain and being in pain. I realized that relaying my capacity to feel pain, I should also strive to reveal my ability for feeling and embracing joy.

This realization took me back to Stevie Wonder's "Joy Inside My Tears" and why I'm writing this book. Diana's appropriation of "If It Makes You Happy" to show her affection for Lee reminded me of the line I quoted from Wonder's "Joy Inside My Tears." Her devotion to Lee and "If It Makes You Happy" displayed the indelible mark that Lee had made on Diana's life history. It reiterated my belief that while the artists may make the music, they aren't necessarily the ones who make it memorable.

21. "THRILLER" / Michael Jackson

Unless one of her "husbands" (Billy Ocean or Lionel Richie) was on-screen, Mom mostly fell in and out of sleep during the Saturday replay of *Friday Night Videos*. Her head swiveled in a slumbering circle that grew increasingly precarious with each forward tilt. Were it not for her snoring drowning out the TV, I would have been indifferent toward Mom's naps. I often resorted to praying for the phone to ring, for Dad to come home so that she'd join him in the kitchen—anything to abate her snoring. Most of all I pined for one of Michael Jackson's videos to come on so that she would wake up and see me do what I do best and show her why everyone in school called me the "Haitian Dancing Machine."

Okay, since I hope some of my friends from elementary school are reading this book, no one ever called me the "Haitian Dancing Machine." But *sheeeit* . . . if New Edition's

"Candy Girl" was on the radio or Jackson's "Billie Jean" video was on the screen, I was badder than Deney Terrio in a pair of gold hot pants. Back in '83 and '84, when I was between the ages of seven and eight, I made the worn green carpet in Mom's bedroom glitter as brilliantly as the fabricated urban sidewalks of the "Billie Jean" video.

When I performed for her, Mom liked humming along—"Toom, toom . . . Toom, toom"—to further inspire me as I pranced across the floor. Coming to a halt I stuck my right leg out and tugged on my brown corduroy pants to reveal my pristine white tube sock. Within an instant that same leg flashed in the air, completing a leg kick that the King of Pop himself would've been proud of. The only thing missing from my repertoire was the toe stand that Jackson executed with the flair of a ballet soul rebel. Jackson could spin around and then come to a complete stop on the tip of his toes. Meanwhile, I had to hold on to either the wall or the door if I tried to complete the move. Being the gracious spectator that she was, Mom would shout out, "I ain't gonna say nothin' when you fall flat on your face and break your teeth."

Although I knew his dance routines better than I did my spelling words, it wasn't until I got older that I learned to fully appreciate "Billie Jean" and the rest of *Thriller*. As a kid, I was captivated by Jackson's aura, celebrity, and dance moves more than his talent as a musician/singer. I thought Michael Jackson was the black Beatle. He was Elvis Presley and Marilyn Monroe rolled into one. As I watched Jackson wading in the tarn of American celebrity, it never occurred to me that *Thriller* was one of the greatest albums of all time. It contains classics like "P.Y.T. (Pretty Young Thing),"

"Human Nature," "Wanna Be Startin' Somethin'," "Beat It," and "Thriller."

Jackson instructed me on how to dress. I was begging Mom to buy me suits, bow ties, and dress shoes when days earlier I'd have done anything and everything to avoid wearing any one, much less all three, of those garments. The other guys and I talked about Jackson as if he was a big brother. In hindsight, though, I think I had a crush on Michael Jackson. He was so easy on the eyes that I rarely remember being as taken with his voice as I was by the sight of him. Even when I listened to him on the radio, I rarely thought about any of the technical merits of his songs. Instead, I envisioned him doing one of his dance routines or fantasized about other smattering images of his buttery brown skin, bashful smile, and lithe body that brought to mind martial artist Bruce Lee. Jackson's performance at Motown's twenty-fifth anniversary extravaganza in May 1983 was his version of the *Mona Lisa*. After performing a medley of Motown-era Jackson 5 classics with his brothers, Michael remained onstage as his brothers scampered off. Pandemonium erupted in the auditorium with the first tap of the snare drum. Before he uttered a single "Billie Jean" verse, Jackson had already received a standing ovation for simply sliding into a modified cat stance. I was mesmerized by his attire: black dress loafers and dress pants, topped off by a glittering button-down shirt, sports jacket, and socks—yes, socks. Long before B.G. and those of his crew from New Orleans, the Cash Money Millionaires, had a whole generation talking about "bling bling," Jackson stunned the world by simply letting the hem of his pants run a little high. Jackson was blinging so hard with his socks that he probably even made Liberace blush. He danced like Fred Astaire, sang like Jackie Wilson, had the suave good looks of a young Sam Cooke, and dressed like Liberace, all of which combined to reinforce the fact that his very existence was a performance in and of itself.

My own performances became the center of some controversy at home. My parents struggled to find a way to help me improve my declining grades and avoid being left back. At first they discontinued my TV privileges, all but putting an end to my Jackson impersonations, and then, at the suggestion of my teacher, got a tutor to help me with my spelling and vocabulary homework. They enlisted one of our teenage neighbors, Seegra, to help me with my homework.

I'd known Seegra and her family from the neighborhood but hadn't really spent any considerable amount of time with them before our tutoring sessions. At first our interactions were awkward; it was my first time working with a tutor and Seegra's first time working with someone as young as me. Making matters worse, the time I spent with her progressed from a more limited interaction to being in her presence five days a week. She essentially became a babysitter and big sister as I became immersed in her family life.

We really began making progress once she homed in on my interests in dancing and performing. Oftentimes before starting a tutoring session, she'd play some music for me to dance to or we'd sing along together as we ate sandwiches and chatted. Once we became more familiar with each other, I grew to appreciate Seegra's commitment to having me figure out the answers for myself rather than just giving them to me whenever I got stuck. Within weeks I had risen to being one of the top spellers in my class. The risk of getting left back was abated for that term.

The third grade got off to an auspicious beginning, but my success was soon derailed when I lapsed back into poor studying habits. My parents didn't give a second thought to enlisting Seegra for more tutoring sessions, and this time there was no resistance on my part. While the tutoring sessions were the same, the extracurricular time that I spent with her lacked the levity of our first series of tutoring sessions. A cousin of hers from Florida named Reed had moved in with her family to finish his last year of high school and to break into the music industry. He and Seegra were always arguing because Reed liked playing big brother to her even though he was barely a year older.

Seegra and I still managed to have our fun, though, and during one of these goof-off sessions she asked if I'd act out Michael Jackson's "Thriller" video with her. She played Michael and I was the Vincent Price character. She cued the record and as soon as I heard the sound of the casket opening, I did a series of wolf howls and then a leg kick. I couldn't really get into this routine because neither the song nor the video appealed to me. Jackson's collaboration with director John Landis on "Thriller" was revolutionary because instead of doing a traditional music video, they created a short film. Unfortunately I have never liked horror movies, so when the zombies flooded the screen, my remaining bits of attention receded almost as quickly as the actress running away from Jackson.

Seegra and I had no chance of keeping up with Jackson for the entire song, and about halfway into "Thriller" she and I collapsed on the couch. Reed walked in from work a few moments later. Usually he went straight to his room, but for some reason he felt social that day and started talking with us. After we filled him in on what had just happened, he told us to wait a second and then jetted out of the living room and into his room. When he came back out, he had his keyboard in tow. "Y'all wanna see somethin'?" he asked as we suppressed our usual urge to giggle at his Southern accent.

"Sure," Seegra said.

Reed started playing "Thriller" and tinkering with the melody by incorporating other sound effects available on his keyboard where the sound of owls howling, caskets closing, and doors slamming normally appear. I was captivated by what Reed could produce with his gadget, and moved over from where I was sitting next to Seegra to sit beside him so I could get a better look at what he was doing. "Thriller" may have been anticlimactic on-screen, but seeing someone play the score in person held my attention. I wanted to see what other songs Reed could replicate on his keyboard.

"Go on, press a key and see what happens," he encouraged. I didn't hesitate, amusing myself with my own off-key musical creations.

Then Seegra asked Reed if he could watch me while she ran to the library to get a book for school. He and I both knew this was her code for sneaking out to see her boyfriend. He agreed.

I thought she had forgotten something inside the house when she reopened the door. Instead she stuck her head in, and said, "Ferentz, don't tell your parents about this, okay?

I'll bring you back some candy if you promise to keep this a secret. Bet?"

"Bet," I replied.

Reed continued letting me use his keyboard as he went off to his room. He came out about twenty minutes later and plopped himself down on the couch, practically falling on top of me. "Having fun?" he asked.

"Yeah," I replied, barely taking my eyes off the keyboard.

After a few minutes of staring at me as I played with the keyboard, Reed asked if I could do my Michael Jackson routine for him.

I refused.

"How you gonna diss me like that?" he said. "I let you use my keyboard and then you gonna say no when I ask you a favor. That's really foul. If you gonna be like that I'm going to take my joint and go back into my room with it."

Thinking that he might be serious, I agreed to do the routine: "Just once."

I did the same "Billie Jean" routine that I used to do in my mom's room.

After I finished Reed asked if I could do the "Thriller" routine with him because he was planning on performing it in a talent show and needed the practice. At first he asked if he could play Michael. As he went through his routine, we were both cracking up, and when the Vincent Price portion came on I jumped up and started mimicking Price's lines. We were both into the scene when he asked if we could do it one more time, and I obliged. He'd be Michael again, but this time he wanted me to be the girl.

The girl? Hell no, I thought.

"No!" I said. He pleaded some more and I held firm to my position and sat on the couch. When he turned on the song again, I paid him no attention, and before I knew it he was on my lap holding down my arms as I tried to push him off. The more I tried to move, the more Reed exerted his weight on me; in an instant I felt his lips on mine. I began to spit as much as possible while I swiveled my head from side to side. Then he punched me in the chest, setting off a coughing fit. At this point Reed got off me and turned the volume on the stereo louder as I lay on the couch crying. I tried leaving the apartment but he pulled me back in.

"I was just playing around," he said. "If you didn't move your head so wildly, I would have never kissed you." He then took his hand and put it over my lips and placed a kiss on the back of his hand. "That's all that I was going to do," he went on. "Just like in the movies."

Reed was right. It was my fault for moving around too much. For not cooperating. For messing up the scene. Maybe it was fear, maybe it was naïveté, maybe it was shame. Honestly, I don't know what it was that made me nod my head "yes" when at the end of his speech Reed told me, "Don't tell anyone, okay? This is just between the two of us."

Giving Reed the benefit of the doubt that first time, I didn't tell anyone what had happened. Maybe he was right. If I had just stopped being such a baby, I would be able to see what an innocent joke he was trying to play. Weeks went by without any other incidents. Seegra left him alone with me only once more during that time so she could take a quick run to the supermarket. Reed also got more hours at his part-time job at a music shop, further decreasing his time at the house.

I was surprised to find that Reed was the only one home one day when I arrived at Seegra's apartment after school. He told me that she had to stay after school to take her yearbook picture and wouldn't get home until five thirty at the earliest. Since my parents weren't home and I didn't have keys, I had no other option but to stay and wait for her. When I came inside, Reed left me alone in the living room to watch TV and went off to his bedroom. About thirty minutes later he came out to the living room and asked me if what Seegra had told him about me saying that I could put him in wrestler Ken Patera's patented full nelson and he wouldn't be able to escape was true.

Not paying him much attention, I mumbled, "Yeah, I said it."

"What'd you say?" he shouted from across the room. "Don't you know how to talk like a man?"

"I said, 'Yeah, I said it!'" I shouted back.

"Well, let's see you do it then," he cast back at me. He moved the coffee table aside to give us a ring in which to wrestle. In spite of the fact that he was almost ten years older than me, I thought I could outwrestle him. The "Thriller" incident was still in the back of my mind, and I thought that this was a chance to get even with him. If I could manage to inflict some pain on Reed, then he would know how I felt that day when he pounced on me.

I asked him to get on his knees so that I would have the necessary leverage to lock my arms around his shoulders. As soon as I locked my fingers, he would simply flex his arms downward and break out of the hold. All of my adjustments were proving futile and Reed had made his point: I was too weak to put him in a hold. Yet toward the end of our experiment, he conceded to the full nelson and acted as if I had put him in a painful position. I bought it. Just when I began feeling happy about my accomplishment, he flipped me over his shoulder, causing me to do a somersault in the air and land flat on my back. As I squirmed in pain, Reed jumped on top of my chest and pinned my arms down underneath his knees. My squirming turned to all-out tears as he bore his weight down on my biceps. Before I knew it he had opened his pants and had begun whipping me across the face with his penis.

My crying only made him angrier. With each cry he ground his knees down on my arms and his butt on my chest. I felt as if I was going to choke under all his weight. He just kept yelling, "Shut up!" As my cries grew louder he got up and turned on the radio to drown them out. When he got back from adjusting the radio, he picked me up off the ground by my collar and dragged me into his room toward the back of the apartment. I fought as much as I could, pulling things down as we passed by tables and trying to make myself dead weight.

Once we got inside his room, he threw me on his bed. I instantly rolled off, pulling the sheets with me. He punched me in the stomach. Throughout I kept on screaming, hoping someone would help me. To shut me up, he put a pillow over my face and began trying to unbuckle my pants. I kicked as violently as I could. He gave up on this mission, but after lifting the pillow, he again flashed his penis in front of my face, running it over my mouth. I managed to wrangle myself off the bed again and broke for the door.

When I got outside, I had nowhere to run. My parents weren't home and I didn't have keys to get inside the house.

A family friend saw me in our building's lobby and asked me what had happened. I told him that Reed had been beating me up, at which point he consoled me and told me that he was sure that Reed was just playing. By this time Reed had collected himself and found me talking to this man. He said we had just been wrestling, that he had been teaching me how to fight. I continued to whimper as Reed explained the situation to our neighbor. Believing Reed, our neighbor told me that Reed was just trying to toughen me up and that as a boy I would need to be tough.

Thankfully the family friend let me stay at his house until my mother got home, and he told her what had happened. I tried explaining the truth to my mom . . . but trying to do so in Kreyol, not knowing the words for everything and feeling afraid of using profanity in front of my mother, I focused my story on the wrestling, the punching, and the beating. My mom then told me not to wrestle with Reed anymore because he was older and bigger than I was. The next day she had a set of keys made for me just in case Seegra wasn't home again.

My tutoring sessions with Seegra continued off and on until I was in the fifth grade. Reed had moved out after I finished the third grade, but he came back to visit twice a year. Whenever he visited, Seegra's parents would have me over for dinner and afterward I was expected to join Reed and Seegra in a talent showcase. I did my best to avoid doing any scenes that required practicing with Reed.

Long after *Thriller*'s popularity had declined, Seegra's parents would ask for my Jackson routine. It always felt odd doing the routine while Reed was in the room, so instead I told jokes or did some break-dancing. Back then I never connected the molestation with Jackson's music, which I continued to listen to and thoroughly enjoy throughout the eighties. I always thought that my dancing was the culprit.

I have pretty much kept these encounters a secret for most of my life. Prior to the publication of this book, I never told my parents, brother, or any other close family members. The only people I ever told were girlfriends because I felt that otherwise they wouldn't understand my discomfort with being touched, why I would jump or stiffen as soon as I felt their hand on the small of my back or my shoulder. When I initially became sexually active, I shared this story with my then girlfriend in order to explain my apprehensions about sex.

While undergoing counseling in graduate school, I eventually told my psychologist during a second series of sessions after having kept it hidden from him during our first. We explored the effects that keeping this secret for so long had on my life. I told him how being molested made me question myself—my ability to defend myself, my sexuality, and my manliness—for most of my life. These disclosures were cathartic. Each counseling session sparked a new epiphany. I remember one in particular where after discussing a friend's allegations that I was aloof and oftentimes distant, my counselor simply shrugged his shoulders and said, "It makes sense, doesn't it, considering what you've been through."

At first I was taken aback by how casually he delivered his reply. Having grown accustomed to being coddled by girlfriends who were afraid of hurting me whenever I disclosed being molested, I never knew what it felt like to discuss this matter in a setting where those anxieties were suspended. It felt normal. My head didn't explode and the world as I know it didn't end.

He then added, "I'm less concerned with what your friends think of you than I am with what you think of yourself." I had spent so much time anticipating other people's reactions to this revelation that I wasn't taking time to address what it meant to me. My counselor's comment prompted me to realize that I was ashamed of myself. Until I was able to overcome this sense of shame, I had to be prepared for people misinterpreting how I related to them because of the way I was defining my relationship with myself.

This process of letting go was disturbed when the recurring child abuse allegations against Michael Jackson intensified during the fall of 2003, the same time that I started outlining what became *Songs in the Key of My Life*. Prior to 2003, I did not know what to make of the suits leveled against Jackson. Was he as innocent as the various acquittals suggested, or were these just another series of examples of how money inevitably trumps justice? What was the purpose of discussing how "Thriller" has been instrumental in my life?

It took three years for me to figure out that this chapter is about silence. It's about the silence I have maintained during countless discussions with friends about the allegations leveled against Jackson. It's about when in trying to figure out whether I am being too personal and exposing too much about myself in a talk, I end up saying nothing at all. This chapter is about the silence that I pray will end when someone else reading this realizes, like I did, that he or she isn't alone.

22. "BORN IN THE U.S.A." /
Bruce Springsteen

When Bruce Springsteen's single "Born in the U.S.A." was released, Michael Jackson was the most recognizable celebrity in the world. Jackson was unable to go anywhere without getting mobbed, regardless of whether he was stepping out of his house in California or off an airplane in Cairo. In spite of his celebrity and the overwhelming success of *Thriller*, I still never recall any one of Jackson's songs touching a nerve quite like Springsteen's "Born in the U.S.A." did.

"Born in the U.S.A." wasn't merely ubiquitous—like, for example, Cyndi Lauper's "Girls Just Want to Have Fun." There was a major movement to make "Born in the U.S.A." a permanent fixture in this nation's history.

I was eight years old when Springsteen's album *Born in the U.S.A.* was released. It features seven top-ten singles, a record matched only by *Thriller* and Janet Jackson's *Rhythm*

Nation 1814. Interestingly enough, it was the somber meditation on a city coming apart at the seams, "My Home-
town," that went to the top of the charts, with "Dancing in
the Dark" being the only other song from the album to
reach as high as number two. "Born in the U.S.A." made it
to the ninth spot, a surprisingly low number considering
how omnipresent of a single it seemed to be.

Despite the common associations made with "U.S.A."—
images of large audiences at everything from professional
wrestling matches to political rallies fervently waving flags—
the song presents a bleak outlook on life in the United
States. Springsteen homes in on the experience of a Vietnam veteran returning to the United States only to find it
not as welcoming as he'd imagined.* This veteran comes
from a small town—or in Springsteen's words, "a dead man's
town"—where he is unable to find work at the local refin-
ery and is abandoned to reside

> *Down in the shadow of the penitentiary*
> *Out by the gas fires of the refinery . . .*

The allusion to the penitentiary reiterates the veteran's
prevailing feelings of being trapped in the United States. In
an earlier verse in the song, the veteran declares that he enlisted in the war because he felt trapped and defeated in his
own country.

The veteran finds himself "stuck at home," devoid of the

*Sylvester Stallone's 1982 film *First Blood* features a similar protagonist,
John Rambo. In spite of the film's earlier release date, records indicate
that Springsteen had composed "Born in the U.S.A." before *First Blood*
premiered.

American free spirit that Springsteen romanticized in one of his earlier albums, *Born to Run* (1975). As "Born in the U.S.A." draws closer to its conclusion, we find Springsteen reconsidering his previous youth anthem as his current narrator comes to grips with living in the jail that fighting in Vietnam was supposedly going to help him evade.

This dreary narrative is a departure from the images of enthusiastic patriotic audiences waving their flags as "Born in the U.S.A." played in the background. What often comes to mind when I think of this song is the sight of wrestler Hulk Hogan defeating either Nikolai Volkov or the Iron Sheik, who in professional wrestling grudge matches represented U.S. enemies Russia and Iran, respectively. After his victory, Hogan, whose normal theme song was Survivor's "Eye of the Tiger," retrieved a flag from one of the spectators in attendance and proceeded to march across the ring waving it. As he made his way around the ring, "Born in the U.S.A." played through the speakers, which, when coupled with the spectacle Hogan was performing in the ring, further roused the crowd into a frenzy.

I also think of '84 presidential candidates Walter Mondale and Ronald Reagan courting Springsteen's support during their campaigns. Each of them sought to align himself with Springsteen's transcendent chorus as they both eluded honestly engaging its message. As military spending rose in anticipation of the third world war that the United States seemed perpetually on the verge of engaging in during the '80s, many Americans considered Springsteen's anthem a thought-provoking reminder of the disastrous consequences of the last major war in which the United States was involved. Paradoxically, these two politicians thought that by evading its message and amplifying the chorus, they could play on patriotic and nationalist fervor and gain admission into the White House, or, as in the case of Reagan, ready Americans to serve in the cold war. Reagan and Mondale courted Springsteen's endorsement as if he was the second coming of Francis Scott Key and had just updated the national anthem. Springsteen refused to endorse either Reagan or Mondale.

If I sound cynical or bitter, it's because I was one of the people who bought into the patriotic fervor. Three years after I had arrived from Haiti, a Haitian citizen still fumbling through English, I adopted "Born in the U.S.A." as my first favorite song. I eagerly anticipated hearing it on one of the New York radio stations as I got ready for school in the morning. Upon hearing it, or rather its chorus, I somehow felt better equipped to tackle the challenges that lay ahead of me that day: the kids teasing me about my weight, accent, supposed Haitian body odor (HBO), and—what was becoming a more common point of attack—the odds of me having AIDS. After all, didn't all Haitians have AIDS?

I spent three years feeling as if my struggles could have been alleviated if I were American. I'd be a better student from the outset if I was fluent in English. Kids at school would have less ammunition to pick on me because I wouldn't naïvely back into the punch lines of their jokes. Finally, my relationship with my parents, in particular my father, wouldn't be antagonistic because they couldn't chide me for being slow to learn English.

In "Born in the U.S.A." I found my streets paved with

gold. It represented my foundation for this preeminent immigrant-American myth. It was the magic bullet to relieve me of my foreigner's afflictions.

In that sense, I made the same investment in "Born in the U.S.A." that Americans of all stripes seemed to be making in the song. I was as misguided as Reagan and the conservatives who treated the song like it was a pep rally anthem. It makes sense that as an eight-year-old I was seduced by the song's chorus into wanting to join the cavalcade of flag-waving supporters. What's disturbing, however, is how so many adults who were fluent in English could have misinterpreted "Born in the U.S.A." and completely ignored the story relayed through the lyrics. The disregard shown for the plight of Springsteen's soldier probably helps explain why in less than twenty years this country went from touting its artists as patriots to targeting them through the Patriot Act, and why so many of us are still trailing the rapture when we need to be heeding the message.

23. "FINGERTIPS" / *Stevie Wonder*

Just as religious pilgrimages are an opportunity for people of the same faith to gather in celebration of their principles, the party promoter KeiStar Productions' annual celebration, WONDER-Full, offers Stevie Wonder enthusiasts a chance to pay "tribute to the genius of Stevie Wonder." As with many religious observations, WONDER-Full happens at the same time every year in New York City, the Saturday closest to May 13, Wonder's birthday. Many of the same people attend it, so every year you're practically guaranteed to run into a friend you haven't seen since last year's party while waiting on line outside the club. The party itself, with all the dancing and applauding, is actually more like a revival, which probably explains why, by attending WONDER-Full over the past four years, I transitioned from agnostic Wonder listener to a jubilant Wonder fan.

WONDER-Full is at its best when it's teeming with people dancing to host Bobbito Garcia and DJ Spinna's selections. Five hundred people on a dance floor with their arms raised in the air and sweat dripping down their bodies who are as energetic at 3:00 AM. as they were at 10:00 PM is an astounding sight. Concepts such as octave, tone, and register matter very little to this congregation, who take full license to indulge in all the forms of commotion that Wonder's music inspires. I love the feeling of the WONDER-Full crowd when it's communally crying, dancing, shouting, clapping, and stomping to Wonder's songs.

What I love the most is the pandemonium that erupts when Bobbito and Spinna play universal favorites. These songs spur screams throughout the crowd and bring an onrush of people to the dance floor. The last song that I remember inciting this reaction was Wonder's 1963 hit "Fingertips, Pt. 2," his first number-one single from his first chart-topping album, *The 12 Year Old Genius*.

It was about 1:00 A.M. I felt uncharacteristically tired and a bit overwhelmed by the crowd and thought I should call it a night. My friend James and I had spent the last half hour in our allotted four square feet of space on the dance floor, avoiding being trampled by the couples dancing to our right and bobbing and weaving out of the way of the Afro and hyperactive booty-shaking of one of the women in the trio to our left. I was all set to give James a pound and head toward the door when these bongo-drum taps elicited yells from everyone around me.

All three of the women on my left threw their arms up in unison. The couples on my right switched from their uptempo romantic two-step with their foreheads pressed against each other to a more frenetic dance. They clapped their hands as if they were patting a tambourine and rocked from side to side like ecstatic swing dancers. This sudden burst of energy threatened to entrap James and me even further in our little space. However, with Wonder instructing everyone to "stomp your feet, clap your hands, jump up and down" and do whatever else we wanted, this speck of space that felt stifling during the previous song, "Love Light in Flight," now felt like a wide-open territory. "Fingertips" was lubricating our limbs and everyone was moving freely.

Folks trampolined up and down, making the third floor of Club Shelter feel as if it had somehow been transformed into a mosh pit, except we weren't slamming into one another. We bathed in our unintentional contact. I stopped concentrating on wiping my brow and just let the sweat fall.

As I pulled my shirt away from my body so that my skin could get some air, I noticed that James's T-shirt was pasted to his abdomen. Drenched in perspiration, James's brown T-shirt looked dark red under the hazy neon lights. We both looked as if we were about to fall out. Yet like me, the sweatier that James got, the wider the grin on his face grew.

Dancing to the brink reminded me of watching my father tossing my little brother in the air as a Wonder song like "Signed, Sealed, Delivered I'm Yours," played in the background when I was a little kid. With each heave, Randy was thrown higher into the air until his heels were practically bouncing off the ceiling. And with each heave, he became even more inebriated with glee.

Twenty-five years later, as I sat in a cab, still on my "Fingertips" high, my mind drifted back to more memories of when I first came to the United States from Haiti at the age of five. It reminded me of the days when the only way I knew how to show my appreciation or understanding of a song was to dance.

During those first years in apartment 1F in Jamaica, Queens, I didn't know a lick of English. I was becoming acquainted with my parents, whom I had just met after living with my grandparents in Haiti. Back then, Dad was "Papi Franz" and Mom was "Mami Clo." I hated practicing English with them, but I loved conjuring up dance routines for them at night. After about an hour or so I'd take a break and lie down at the foot of their bed as I tried conjuring dances to perform, but somehow that break always seemed to end up lasting late into the night. The next morning I'd find myself in my bed without any idea how I got there.

The euphoria of "Fingertips" summoned memories of sneaking into the kitchen as Mom prepared dinner and jamming at the table to "Part-Time Lover." I'd take off my plastic-rim glasses, replacing them with a pair of dark Ray-Ban sunglasses that someone had left in my dad's cab. Firmly positioned in front of my imaginary keyboard, I got Mom's attention by tapping on the table. As I swayed from side to side, Mom looked over her shoulder, but quickly turned back around, acting as if my commotion was of little interest to her. We both knew that she was already giggling. I ratcheted up my tapping on the table, repeating what I considered the refrain—"part-time lover, part-time lover"—even louder.

She had on this white housedress with a floral print. Her pressed curls bounced up and down on the back of her shoulders as she joined me by humming along. I can still hear her plastic slippers tapping against linoleum tiles. I will always relish the smell of *boulette*, Haitian meatballs, in the frying pan that sent a flurry of onion, tomato, cayenne pepper, basil, thyme, and rosemary scents scurrying across our apartment. When the song was fading out, Mom cocked her head back and let out the laugh that she'd been suppressing. Without looking directly at me she'd say, "So now you think you're Stevie Wonder."

That scene from twenty-odd years ago feels as recent as last year's WONDER-Full party. It reminds me of what Wonder's music has always meant to me. With these thoughts running through my head during the cab ride, I realized that the craying was over. I was once again causing some commotion. I was once again dancing.

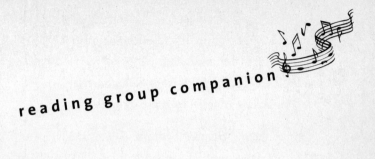

reading group companion

Songs in the Key of My Life charts the coming-of-age of a young Haitian immigrant in New York City. Using a variety of songs as signposts, the author maps out a turbulent childhood that leads him into a self-defining adulthood. The questions that follow are meant to spark discussion about the impact of popular culture, love, faith, and spirituality on becoming an adult.

1. In the introduction, Ferentz compares Tricia's mother's tales about growing up in Detroit to his mom's stories about life in Petionville. What are some of the stories about music that have been passed down in your family, or stories that you look forward to passing on to forthcoming generations?

2. Immediately upon arriving in New York, Ferentz's parents used television and music to ease his transition from Haitian culture to American culture. Why is he so drawn to American cultural icons such as wrestling and heavy metal? How is his ability to relate to his schoolmates affected by these interests?

3. In the second chapter, Ferentz rewrites the lyrics to "Caribbean Queen" for his first love, Adriana. What do you remember about your first love? What songs come to mind when you think of her or him?

4. Happiness is a major theme in this book. The lack of it prompts Tricia to end their engagement, and the pursuit of it inspires Ferentz to write this book. Happiness also comes up when he's discussing "If It Makes You Happy," when he's dancing, and, of course, with "Romie." What about music makes you happy, and are there any songs in particular that are guaranteed to bring a smile to your face?

5. In the chapter "Thriller," why does Ferentz choose to wrestle with Reed? Why is the author able to hold on to the Michael Jackson songs even though they underscore his molestation? Has he come to terms with his sexual abuse? How much of that experience still plays out in his adult life?

6. Ferentz proposes some interesting connections between adolescence, war, and music in the chapter "Me So Horny." Do you agree with his connections? How do you think the connections he draws between war,

politics, and music relate to similar connections in the chapter "Born in the USA"?

7. In "As"/"You Are My Heaven" Ferentz reiterates that *Songs in the Key of Life* was at the center of his relationship with Tricia. Is there a current or past serious relationship of yours that had a similar relationship to an album? What was the album and how and why did you and your lover grow to appreciate it so much?

8. Why does Ferentz revisit his relationship with God? What are your thoughts on his view that people are searching for definition as much as they are salvation? Are there any songs that you might have used in place of "Jesus Walks" if you were writing this chapter?

9. How much of a role does music play in the healing process for Ferentz? What specific moments in the memoir show it to be a balm? Do you use music as healer? What songs or artists do you turn to in times of need or support? What is it about those songs that soothes you?

10. Which song would you pick as your favorite out of the many that Ferentz has discussed in the book? Why? What memories and feelings do you associate with that song?

11. What does Stevie Wonder's legacy mean to you? Name three of your favorite Stevie tracks. Why are they your favorites?

Here are some fun music-related exercises that reading group members can incorporate into their *Songs in the Key of My Life* experience.

1. Stevie Wonder's lyrics can often double as poems. Similarly, Ferentz Lafargue inserts some poetry of his own into the prose of *Songs in the Key of My Life*. Choosing one of the songs from the book or, if you prefer, another one important to your own life, write a short poem that reflects your feelings about the song or a moment/person that you always connect with this song. Afterward, each book club member will share his or her poem and talk briefly about the feelings that he or she sought to convey and how those feelings relate to the chosen song.

2. Create a sound track for your book club. Each member selects one song that best captures the feelings inspired from participating in the club or from a particularly memorable session. Send the song to a preappointed person who will compile all the songs on a CD mix. The songs should not be forwarded to all the members of the group but only to this one person, who can be either a club member or nonaligned third party. Listen to the CD mix straight through either at the beginning of your meeting or at the end, and while everyone listens have each member try to guess who selected each of the songs on the CD. A prize can be given to the member who gets the most songs correct. Then go around the room and have

everyone discuss why the particular song they chose encapsulates their feelings about the club.

3. A simple exercise would be to have your book club discussion surrounded by music. Have whoever's hosting the group gather a list of favorite songs from club attendees and create a CD or MP3 list that will serve as background music to the discussion. Invariably, folks will light up when they hear "their song" and can talk about why it means so much to them.

4. In "As"/"You Are My Heaven," Ferentz indicates that his and Tricia's objective in creating the musical registry for their wedding was to compile an "African diaspora soul shakedown." The music from Africa and its diasporas, such as Haiti, Jamaica, and Nigeria, have played a major role in Ferentz's journey. Choose one or a few of the African and African diaspora countries mentioned and ask the members of your club to bring along musical recordings and culinary dishes from that part of the world for you all to enjoy as you discuss *Songs in the Key of My Life*.

Ferentz Lafargue earned a Ph.D. at Yale University and teaches literature at Eugene Lang College, The New School University. He lives in Brooklyn.